# PUBLIC SERVICE REFORM... BUT NOT AS WE KNOW IT!

A story of how democracy can make
public services genuinely efficient

# Hilary Wainwright
## with Mathew Little

For Jane, who questions everything

*Published by Compass and UNISON with support from the Transnational Institute and the International Centre for Participation Studies, Bradford University and distributed by Picnic Publishing.*

First published in Great Britain 2009 by Picnic Publishing
PO Box 5222, Hove BN52 9LP

A catalogue record for this book is available from the British Library.

ISBN: 9780956037053

Printed and bound in Great Britain by CPI Group
Designed by SoapBox, www.soapboxcommunications.co.uk

# Contents

**Introduction**                                                    7
**Mission impossible?**

**Chapter 1**
**Welcome to Newcastle – the way we were and**     16
**the need for change**
*With a 25-year old IT system and departments operating in
silos, Newcastle council is stuck in the past. Its back office functions are remote from the needs of service users and change is
seen as a threat. Although there is a new need to save money
whilst improving services, nobody is leading in-house change.*

**Chapter 2**                                                      32
**'The status quo is not an option'**
*A new Chief Executive of the council wants to bring in the
private sector but trade unions want in-house change. They
commission research, get involved in the procurement
process, take industrial action, reach out to the community
and to councillors. The campaign turns from a technical to a
political issue and with the will and involvement, of the whole
workforce, management included confidence grows in what
could be achieved. The in-house bid is submitted.*

**Chapter 3**                                                      57
**Making it happen**
*The in-house bid wins against the private competition, and
a new management team from inside and outside the council*

*is assembled to implement it. Trade Unions are involved as full partners, and openness is a hallmark of the process from the start.*

## Chapter 4                                            69
### Financial means and constraints

*There are tight targets. A loan is taken out to be repaid as savings are made. Collaboration across the council make the process work – based on the values of a public service culture.*

## Chapter 5                                            78
### A new spirit of public sector management

*Staff who were previously stuck in routine procedures are now relied upon to use their initiative and creativity to provide a complex and personalised service. Managers become coaches not commanders. Risks are understood and assessed, but not avoided. Project management is put in place but used flexibly to get the job done. These changes reveal hidden staff talents.*

## Chapter 6                                            95
### The union: making management accountable to the change

*Unions sign up to the deal and management agree to involve them at every level. Union reps talk to management team candidates and their views are taken into consideration when appointing. A 'no surprises' policy is adopted by both sides with problems solved through discussions, in groups and one-to-one. High levels of union organisation and education proves vital to staff involvement.*

## Chapter 7                                    104
### Employing the private sector on the terms of the public

*Private sector help is called in, but only where it is needed. The IT system is privately provided, but at a 'maximum price' deal which places risk with the provider. Where consultants are used, their expertise is transferred over to permanent council staff.*


## Chapter 8                                    111
### Ch ch ch changes...

*We've got lots of good intentions, well-worked out plans and great ideas, but now we need to look at the practicalities.*

*Part One : Snakes and ladders*                 111

*Change should be fun as well as serious - get rid of the snakes and its easier to climb the ladders; a new contact centre is needed with an ethos of going the extra mile to help people; 'one stop shops' are introduced with integrated IT systems and personal, face to face guidance to give people open and easy access to council services and resources; but some people miss the greater number of neighbourhood housing offices even though their services were fewer and slower.*

*Part Two: the back office – snakes in the dark*    130

*Information systems matter, and without them bills and benefits don't get paid on time and public money is wasted but nobody takes responsibility; 'If it ain't broke don't fix it' won't do, but just ask the staff and they know what needs to change; reducing management layers lets people collaborate with each other to solve problems; and looking in from the outside some changes are so obvious no one knows why they've never been done before.*

*Part Three: A ladder but not of the conventional kind*    142
*A new system for the admin of HR, payroll, training will let managers support staff better; but every department does things in a different way, and everyone has a different level of knowledge; technology can help, but a dedicated project team with lots of autonomy makes sure new systems are designed to help humans make the most of their capacities.*

*Part Four: Revs and Bens: snakes and (eventually) ladders*    149
*Change isn't popular everywhere; its hard to swallow when someone tells you that your management methods for the future; a transparent process and common objectives give something to hold to when change is being forced through.*

## Chapter 9
## The labour pains and potentialities of change    161

*Some jobs have to go but there has been a commitment to avoid compulsory redundancies; pro-active effort is put into training and redeploying staff into areas of growth, giving them 'taster sessions' of working elsewhere; its never easy, but staff know they are being supported.*

## Chapter 10
## Positively public QED

*We're at the end of a journey, but the road carries on. Its time*    167
*to ask some questions. Was it really a success? Let's have a look at the hard evidence. What was at the heart of these changes? What can Newcastle tell us about public services providing choice, empowerment, and personalised services? And in a recession, what can public services do for us?*

# Introduction

## Mission impossible?

One sign of the dismal state of party politics at Westminster and the narrowness of the range of views that have a parliamentary voice is that neither of the two main political parties responsible for the creation of the welfare state seems to believe that public sector staff can improve the services that they deliver. Neither the party of Aneurin Bevan, the minister who oversaw the establishment of the National Health Service, nor the party of William Beveridge, whose wartime report provided the basis for the modern welfare state, pay serious attention to the possibilities for effective reform from within. And the media in general reflect the restricted range of thought of the Westminster village – for them, 'public service reform' means 'marketisation and outsourcing to the private sector'.

The problem here is not that the public sector and public management of public services is working just fine and doesn't need to change. Rather, it is that few political leaders in either of the two parties responsible for founding the welfare state positively promote the idea of public sector staff themselves working with citizens and elected politicians creatively to improve the services that they deliver.

Yet the track record of sub-contracting strategic services to private companies suggests that it is high time that such publicly-led processes of public service reform be taken more seriously. In 2007, the Local Government Association warned that the extent to which local authority spending is tied up in external contracts would make it harder to achieve the latest efficiency targets without damaging services.[1] Independent research in the same year identified 105 outsourced contracts for IT services in central government, the NHS and local authorities that had cost significantly more than in the original contract, or had been delayed or terminated.[2] At the beginning of 2008, an Audit Commission investigation into major long-term contracts between local government and the private sector concluded that anticipated benefits of economies of scale, innovation and risk sharing had not been realised.[3] And a major report commissioned by UNISON on the rise of the multibillion pound private 'public services industry' raised a host of concerns about the government's increasing dependence on private providers, including increased costs, deteriorating quality, loss of accountability and heightened risks of service failure.[4]

In getting government to acknowledge these findings and look to public servants themselves to carry through change, we come up against a profound mental block. For Labour it is a mindset with deep historical roots, going back long before New Labour's recent attraction to private-sector solutions to problems of public service delivery. One of the founders of the Labour Party who laid the foundations of its method of governing and running the public sector was the Fabian intellectual

Beatrice Webb. Discussing how public institutions should be run, she said: 'We have little faith in the "average sensual man". We do not believe that he can do much more than describe his grievances, we do not think he can prescribe his remedies ... We wish to introduce the professional expert.' New Labour governments have adapted this, in effect, to: 'We have little faith in the "average public sector worker" (or manager for that matter). They are part of the problem not the solution ...We wish to introduce the private company ... '

This book challenges this mindset. It does so by asking *how* to bring about internal change? Who will make it happen? Who are the key actors? The story in this book provides one set of answers to these questions – and with it a new common sense. The story of public service reform in Newcastle is about the nitty gritty of improving public services, even under the fierce pressure to make fast, dramatic savings – faster than the leaders of change would have chosen themselves.

Very recently the government has started to talk about empowering public sector workers. 'Energising the workforce,' says the Cabinet Office's Strategy Unit, 'is a key element of the next phase of our reform programme.'[5] We do not know yet what this means in practice – what is involved in a workforce becoming 'energised' by the cause of public service reform; what role the organisations to which most public service workers belong, public sector trade unions, might play in the process; and how government policy might support this process. Without such practical understanding, this talk runs the risk of being

9

mere rhetoric, remote from the day-to-day realities of public service delivery for a workforce demoralised by cycle after cycle of reform initiatives done *to* them rather than *with* them, let alone led *by* them.

This book recounts the story of a workforce that seems to have 'energised' itself through playing an active part in a well organised branch of UNISON. Between 2000 and 2002, this union and these workers successfully resisted the outsourcing to the private sector of Newcastle City Council's corporate 'back office' and customer services, and then worked closely with management to see through an 'in-house' plan for improving services.

The people whose story you will read here provide, maintain and develop Newcastle Council's ICT infrastructure. They process and deliver housing and council tax benefits, and run the council's exchequer service – paying and chasing debts, administering its payroll and personnel systems and running its 'one stop' customer service centres. Since the successful union-led campaign and in-house bid against the proposed private sector takeover of these services from the council, they are now integrated in a new council department, known as 'City Service'.[6]

The successful in-house bid laid the basis for a transformation led by local government managers who believed in the creative capacities and commitment of council staff and made this the basis of improving services to the public and making savings that were allocated to frontline services for adult social care. Fundamental to turning this into a strategy that delivered improvements in the quality of the services alongside £34.5 million gross savings[7] over eleven and a half years has been the positive involvement of the local UNISON branch. The foundation for this involvement was laid by the union's successful campaign for an in-house bid in the procurement process. The branch had a strong influence on the vision of transformation presented by this in-house bid. It committed itself to the transformation on the basis of there being no compulsory redundancies and then supported and represented its members in the process of change.

The role of a powerful union branch with a strategically minded leadership and a highly active and well-briefed membership is a distinctive feature of the Newcastle story but it is a role that is integral to the whole and very difficult to isolate at every point in the process. A bit like a crucial ingredient to make a special dish, you can't necessarily trace its path at every stage.

We are talking here about a paradigm shift for the reform of public service. Yet despite the change in mindset that it entails, it's really quite straightforward. When you read this story you'll see that, in essence, it's a common-sense approach to public service reform that has been understood in practice by many public sector workers, managers and trade unionists but must be pressed insistently upon the elected representatives who can take the political decisions to make it possible.

## Why it matters beyond the banks of the Tyne

The extent and pace of privatisation of public services is not widely recognised. It is increases in public spending that tend to get the publicity, from media friend and foe alike. Yet some 20-30% of government spending on public services now goes to the private sector, in total around £80 billion a year according to the government's own assessment. This first exploded in the 1980s under Tory policies of compulsory competitive tendering but has continued apace under New Labour. Public attention has focused on the introduction of private providers to the NHS and education through independent sector treatment centres (ISTCs), polyclinics, and Private Finance Initiative (PFI) hospitals and schools, but the process is perhaps furthest advanced in local government, where the private sector now delivers the majority of social care services and almost half of waste, street cleaning and leisure services.[8]

The privatisation of IT and related corporate services or 'business processes' that Newcastle was faced with is spreading throughout the country.[9] This is partly being driven by the demand from central government for 'efficiency savings'. Following the 2004 Gershon review, all authorities were required to show efficiency savings of 2.5% a year, part of which could be reinvested in new services. For the period 2008-09 to 2011-12 the government is asking for 3% annual cash savings – in effect, requiring authorities to live within ever tighter budgets. In late 2008 the government responded to the shortfall in tax revenues resulting from the financial crisis and consequent recession by cutting back projected budgets even more tightly – insisting on a further £5 billion 'efficiency savings' after 2010, and identifying 'back office operations' as a key target for cuts.

This is a controversial and arguably damaging policy,

rooted in the reluctance of central government to raise sufficient tax revenues to meet rising demands for key services (or empower local authorities to raise their own resources) – but as things stand councils are having to live within it. Frequently, they resort to outsourcing because private companies promise to deliver such savings by bringing in new investment and slashing labour costs. The assumption is that in-house services could never be transformed to match the savings offered by the private sector.

The Newcastle experience is of national and international importance because it shows that – contrary to New Labour's criticism of and lack of confidence in local government – public sector managers and staff can drive and lead change, generating innovative ideas and successfully implementing them. Moreover, they can contract private businesses to work to their agenda on tasks and terms determined by democratically accountable public bodies.

This book comes out at a time when the government assumes that market competition is the necessary spur to the improvement of public services. It demonstrates that this assumption is wrong: that a deepening and strengthening of democracy and a reinvigoration of public service values can be the most appropriate spur to real improvement in how public goods are provided. A robust model of public business that aims for maximum public benefit in its use of taxpayers' money is very different in its priorities and values from a private business model based on the maximisation of profit but it

13

does adopt an approach to the management of public money that doesn't take taxpayers for granted.

There is no doubt that local government *had* often become stuck in its ways, unresponsive and cut off from the changing needs and desires of the citizens that paid its wages. Newcastle City Council was no exception and its back-office services – depending on an antiquated IT server for processing benefits and revenues, administering the payroll, paying suppliers and responding to citizens' queries and problems – were among the worst offenders. But to turn to private business as the stimuli to change was unnecessary.

Clearly, democracy as we have known it – the election of representatives to manage public bureaucracies, local and national – hasn't been entirely up to the job. Embedded routines, departmental empires and stalemated industrial relations have all too often blocked the changes that citizens desire. The vote has not, on its own, been powerful enough to act as a driving force for change.

So this story is also a search: exploring how stronger mechanisms of democracy and responsiveness, including in the nature of public management itself and the strategies of public service trade unions, can open up the running of public services so that citizens – as individuals or as organised groups – can themselves be the stimuli to change. It's a story with lessons for *all* the public sector.

# Introduction

1   *Efficiency in the CSR07*, Local Government Association, 2007

2   *Research Report 3*, Dexter Whitfield, European Services Strategy Unit. December 2007

3   *For Better, For Worse: Value for Money in Strategic Service Delivery Partnerships*, Audit Commission January 2008. For an analysis of the limitations of this report, see *Public Private Partnerships: Condienal 'Research'*, Dexter Whitfield, European Service Strategy Unit, January 2008

4   *The Rise of the 'Public Services Industry'*, Paul Gosling, UNISON, September 2008.

5   *Excellence and Fairness: Achieving World Class Public Services*, Cabinet Office Strategy Unit, 27 June 2008, http://www.cabinetoffice.gov.uk/strategy/work_areas/public_services.aspx

6   City Service comprises: the old 'back office' Exchequer, Payroll, Human Resources and Revenues and Benefits Services, previously hung loosely and inefficiently together as IT and Related Services (ITRS), together with six new customer service centres.

7   £28 million net.

8   See Paul Gosling ibid and also the Julius Commission 2008

9   The European Services Strategy Unit database (www.european-services-strategy.org.uk/psro/part-7/psro-ppp-ssp.doc) covers schemes at 36 local authorities, including Liverpool, Glasgow, Edinburgh and Sheffield. NHS trusts are also being encouraged to outsource their corporate functions to a new 'shared services' scheme run in partnership with the private company Xansa

**15**

# Chapter 1

## Welcome to Newcastle – the way we were, and the need for change

Welcome, then, to Newcastle – and welcome, in particular, to 'the Civic', the imposing town hall of dubious architectural taste, whose skyline turns a fluorescent blue at night and whose attractive grounds by day are host to numerous rabbits, as well as to council staff, taking a break, having a smoke and, just occasionally, enjoying the sun.

The Civic serves a medium-sized city of nearly 300,000 people; a city with strong traditions of working-class collective action, both through the historically well-organised workplaces of heavy engineering and shipbuilding and the working-class communities in the neighbourhoods surrounding these traditional industries that now only have a skeletal presence on the Tyne. Scotswood, Wallsend, Byker, Benwell, the East End, the West End – all names with a strong historical resonance – are now sites of both dereliction and change over which people are struggling to find new means of control.

The Civic has played an ambiguous role in these changes. The origin of its grandiose 'castle' architecture lay in the dream-turned-sour of T Dan Smith to achieve for the city a short cut to modernisation through a partnership with ambitious and, as it turned out, corrupt business partners. There have been a series of schemes with other grandiose ambitions, including – most recently – 'Going for Growth' announcing Newcastle as 'a European City of the future'. At the same time thousands look to the Civic for their benefits, for their social care, for the sustenance of a dense network of community and voluntary organisations, for good schools, parks and the upkeep of the city – and, in the case of nearly 11,500 of them, plus their families, their source of income and daily work.

Tell people that you're doing research at the Civic and they'll be interested and sympathetic and give you a mixed collection of stories. They regard it, like an often absent close relation, with a certain affection and identification but at the same time find much of it beyond their control. Invariably, though, they'll have a relation or a friend who works there.

Exploring the building and who works there and talking to them about what it used be like before 'the transformation', as City Service's programme is known, gives you an idea of the problems that the new organisation faced when it first became part of the life of the Civic.

## The last gasps of the past
Go down to the basement of the 'Civic', into the 'dungeon', and there you'll get a sense of the technological side of the problem that Newcastle Council faced with its IT system.

The remnants of the system are still there, breathing their last gasps in the service of the city's magistrates' courts. The noise hits you immediately: a constant drone of air coolers coping with the heat generated by the 25-year-old servers. The room housing them was originally five times its current size, with great rows of servers and tapes whirring on spools. You can still see stacks of white tapes – the kind they would display for dramatic effect in old James Bond films to show how the secret service, or its current enemy, was deploying the latest computer technology. Here, in the Civic's dungeon, they serve out their final years storing and processing information for the local courts.

Graham Parker worked for 17 years in this room; he was a shift leader. He and his team of four worked in it all hours of the day and night, weekends as well as weekdays. 'Noisy,' he remembers. 'And no windows. But always kept clean. And the overtime pay was good.' This was the engine room of the council's IT infrastructure: the ICL mainframe computer.

What was a computer like this doing for the council in the first place? According to those responsible for it, this antique was there originally to store all the council's data on properties and people in the city in a way that made it efficient to send out bills, pay the workforce, or calculate entitlements to housing benefit. This was known as 'batch processing'.

Every day in this room, 12 women working in shifts would key in data they received from the payroll, council tax and housing and benefits 'directorates', or council departments, information about new staff, changes in salary, holiday pay, pensions, council tax bills, business rates, rents, benefits and so on. The night shift would print out piles of folded sheets of paper containing this information and the following day four women would sort and allocate them for return to the relevant directorates. Then, in each directorate, there would be others dividing the piles again for different staff to process.

'We were a family really,' Graham Parker remembers. Alison Lewis, who supervised the 'data processing girls', as she and her colleagues were known, checking the financial information coming from each department against the totals coming out of the council's accounting system, has a similar recollection: 'We were left to our own devices. At times we felt quite isolated but we built up strong bonds.'

Such close personal ties among the workers were bound to make change uncomfortable. But 'we knew we had to change,' says Parker, who now leads the email support team across the council. Alison Lewis now sits at a desk not far from what's left of the old data processing room, in an airy, attractively laid out contact centre, a room with windows overlooking the Civic's garden – and its numerous rabbits. She's doing the same financial control job as in the past but with the new IT system it's just her now. Some of her friends have jobs elsewhere in the council; some took voluntary redundancy. They meet regularly for lunch.

## At the service of a baroque organisation
Another very distinctive group of people with a close relationship to the council's IT system was the dozen or

so programmers and data analysts. Now you can see them all at a glance in an open plan office on the second floor. (Most of City Service works in open offices; they've saved millions on accommodation.) Before the transformation they worked in three teams for the three separate directorates responsible for payroll, council tax and housing and benefits, scattered across the Civic. The idea was to be close enough to each area of work to respond in detail to its needs. The programmers developed the software necessary to meet the requirements of these directorates – each of which had its own finance section and personnel/human resources and IT teams.

All of these directorates dealt with government legislation and one of the tasks they asked of the programmers was to design and amend software to enable them to implement the legislation in their own way. There were also frequent – but fragmented – attempts to update and improve the council's technological capacity. The work of the data analysts involved analysing and organising information in response to requests from the different directorates.

From a technical point of view there was a certain satisfaction in this customised work. 'We had a lot of control,' recalls Colin Anderson, one of the programmers on the old system and now a leading IT analyst for the new in-house IT operation, City Service. The problem was the highly fragmented nature of the organisation, resulting in duplication of work and expertise and unnecessarily high costs.

Each council department operated as a separate organisational world with its own culture and systems. What's more, each of these departments was run on a strictly hierarchical basis – not for nothing were they called 'directorates' – and to keep the hierarchy in place managers required ever more detailed and specific management information. Thus it was not just the technology that posed a problem but the organisation and culture that the IT programmers and analysts used the technology to serve – and which, whether they liked it or not, their work reinforced and embedded.

No one had responsibility for managing and planning the IT services of the council as a whole until 1998. There was no effective way of identifying possible methods of common provision and economies of scale or spotting efficiencies that could be gained by integrating different IT systems. There was no process of allocating resources according to need, including an up-to-date assessment of what the public wanted from the council and their preferred means of getting it. Directorate budgets were worked out on the basis of what had been spent in the past rather than on any fresh forward planning. Management's general assumption over the years had been that change could be incremental, directorate-by-directorate, adapting to new legislation as they went along.

'Investment in technology is driven by past budgets rather than need-driven.' This was how one member of staff summed up one of the problems at a workshop in 2001, when, as part of the campaign for the in-house bid,

21

UNISON got management to sit down with the staff and explore the problem of the IT-related services in the round. If a directorate had a budget for, say, 100 days IT work – usually on the basis of past experience – then the system would allow them to make use of that allowance, no more and no less, whatever the need. This meant that managers of the different directorates tended to use the customised technology to work round any problems, asking Colin Anderson and his colleagues in the three teams of programmers and analysts for 'more bells and whistles' rather than standing back and considering potential new approaches to the organisation of the business as a whole.

In theory, the programmers and analysts could have worked to integrate the different departmental systems but that wasn't how the business was organised. In effect, the customised technology worked to entrench increasingly inefficient, fragmented forms of organisation. According to Fred Stephen, the deputy head of IT at the time and a strong and quietly persistent advocate of change: 'Software was expensively developed or customised to match antiquated clerical practices. Undoubtedly there was cultural resistance to changing the principle of moulding IT to fit "doing things the Newcastle way". This culture was deep rooted.'

For a long time, neither officers nor politicians took the initiative to face up to the problem. Mention 'ITRS' to former Labour council leader Jeremy Beecham and he sighs, recalling the way that 'there was always another million pounds or so needed for updating the main-frame, which was always nodded through'.

Eventually, though, 'we were ready for change,' says a current ICT applications manager. 'The mainframe going wasn't an issue,' she says. 'It was already difficult to recruit people with the skills to work on mainframe computers – although several other councils still had them.'

Nevertheless, the whole IT section, with its highly skilled analysts and programmers and their background in specific, bespoke 'Newcastle systems', was anxious about the transformation. 'We thought we'd be getting deskilled,' says Colin Anderson, about the move to 'off the shelf' packages managed by a single directorate bringing together the council's IT capacity and the core services that it supports. 'In fact, the work is quite rewarding,' he says now.

### 'In a lonely castle'

Climb the cream lino covered steps to the fifth floor in the Civic, and the vast open plan office of exchequer services will appear. There you'll meet some of the 98 staff responsible for processing and paying the bills to the council's suppliers, getting in the money the council is owed, managing the complex payroll and pension system, training and everything else concerning the administrative side of the authority's 'human resources'. Talk to them about the past and what is most striking is the yawning gulf which existed then between managers and the majority of staff whose jobs were very narrowly defined. 'I'd come in in the morning and my work for the day was a repetitive set of tasks. I had no choice and just did what was set out for me,' says one staff member who worked on updating the council's pay roll. Others agreed. The hierarchical structure of the council produced a bias at every level towards a deferment of initiative and responsibility upwards. Information and control was centralised with the management of each directorate; training was out of date. As a result, front-line staff were deprived of the tools and know-how to take the initiative. Indeed, they were not expected to do so and habitually abrogated all decision-making to their seniors.

The consequence in terms of lost opportunity was vividly expressed in the remarkably uninhibited workshop organised by unions and management early in 2001, when one participant bluntly assessed the options for achieving change: 'Buy in the skills or release our potential.' Improved training was also mentioned as an important factor but more important was a change in structure and culture giving staff the scope and support to take the initiative.

Breaking down the barriers that kept everyone 'in their boxes' was also an urgent need. 'We need to see how we fit into the bigger picture,' insisted another member of staff at the 2001 workshop. The fragmentation of work and the resulting invisibility of the wider context is a recurring theme when staff talk about the past. 'I just got on with my little job – calculating sickness pay – as if I was in a lonely castle, unaware of what was happening in the city,' one member of staff who works on salaries told us. 'The different directorates just worked in their own little boxes,' confirmed another.

Remarks such as these make it clear by negative example what is required for the organisation of a council's IT systems to be geared to the needs of the public. Unless staff can see how their work connects, however indirectly, to the bigger picture of public needs and the chain of action needed to meet them, it is difficult for them to be motivated or to give practical meaning to the idea of public service.

From the point of the public, if responding to their needs is reduced to friendliness in the 'front office', with the 'back office' kept in the dark – 'treated as if we had BO,' as one member of the team who chased unpaid council tax put it – that front-office friendliness is little more than PR gloss. You can rely on Geordie good humour to deliver a cheery reception. But what happens then?

Whether someone goes away satisfied, with their claim met, their parking permit in their pocket, their query about a planning development answered, or their concern about their child's school followed through, depends on how far the whole organisation of the council is geared up to be responsive, accessible, open and committed. And that requires a fully integrated back and front office, a shared information system, an absence of inter-departmental rivalries and an outward-looking culture in which frontline staff are encouraged and supported to solve problems themselves or have at their finger tips the means to enable members of the public to talk directly to more specialised members of staff.

## 'Just doing a job'

The self-image of many council departments was that they were separate entities, isolated from the citizens they were serving. The receiving, processing and paying of benefit, with each task done by different people without any rotation and knowledge of each others work or the process as whole, used to epitomise this fragmentation Go down the road from the Civic to the rather down-at-heel tower block, Scottish Life House and meet some of the 120 people who now work in rotation: spending time meeting the public who are making claims, talking to them in the Contact Centre and working in the back office processes the claims. They'll tell you what it used to be like: 'I had the experience of working in an office where people would think that we're not here for the public, we're just in the office doing a job every day,' one former housing benefit worker in Newcastle told us. And as with many other staff, whose years of service frequently stretch into double figures, the way she did her job had barely altered in the 12 years that she'd worked for the council.

This sclerotic approach had seeped into the way the council was perceived by users of its services. 'The council for so many years was set in its ways. We tended to feel that councillors just let the civil servants at the civic centre run things virtually how they wanted to – because the councillors didn't want to get involved or couldn't be bothered,' says Vic Bond, a resident of the Westerhope area of the city.

Structurally, the council used to present a fragmented face to the public. There were 19 different reception points in the Civic Centre, covering services from parking to education. Customers would stalk its corridors looking for the correct reception desk for their inquiry and frequently get lost in the process. Different council services were also limited in how they communicated with each other. Because they used separate computer systems, customers' inquiries or changes of details could only be logged with one department at a time. Someone moving to or within the city would have to visit or phone several different offices and repeat their registration of their personal details several different times in order to fully access services.

The council also had a presence in the community through 21 housing offices spread across the city in former churches, council estates or office blocks. At these offices, local people could pay their rent or report repairs if they lived in a council property. They could also pay council tax bills, seek housing benefit advice or report other problems such as difficulties with neighbours or anti-social behaviour. Some of the offices were a popular means for less mobile residents to contact the council face to face, but in some cases they had only five or six visitors a day.

The council did not run a dedicated contact centre. Instead, individual departments, such as revenues, which was responsible for council tax, would assign back office staff to answer the phones. Customers could only call between 8.30am and 4.30pm. There was no queuing system, so if all phones were busy callers would merely hear the engaged tone and have to keep trying again and again. Nor could the system show the volume of calls received, so that council staff never knew how many people were trying to get through but hanging up. When a new contact centre was opened in March 2006, for the first time it became apparent how long callers were waiting. Up to 40 people at any one time were waiting for an hour to get through.

The flaws didn't stop when the phones were answered. 'It wasn't easy,' says Denton resident Audrey Shakespeare. 'You often didn't get the correct information, they wouldn't put you onto the right department you wanted to get through to. If you went into the local housing office, you didn't get much information out of them. Even if you phoned up you still didn't get quite the information you were looking for.' One reason why, was that the information was all on paper files. They were not available at the neighbourhood offices. They were stored on a whole floor of Scottish Life House and slow to access. The mainframe computer remember, did not have the capacity to organise complex information. The move to the new technology meant all this became electronic and could be accessed by council staff from anywhere.

### Best value?

The problem was not simply saving money. If money had been saved without changing how things were organised the problems would have been compounded.

The problem was how to do things differently. And that meant rethinking an immensely complex system of interactions.

An important move that opened the debate about these problems and about strategies for improvement was a 'best value' study carried out by Fred Stephen as deputy director of IT. Best value was the New Labour government's replacement for compulsory competitive tendering. Potentially it laid the basis for stimulating a new dynamic for public service improvement geared to the goals of the public sector: meeting the needs and desires of the public. It was an early example of the self-scrutiny and challenge that became central to the City Service programme and illustrates a key element in any internal process of public sector improvement. The Chief Executive, however, made it part of the case for turning to the private sector for rescue. Financial crisis also strengthened the pressure for a short-term fix.

## Financial black hole

The expense of the mainframe computer became an urgent issue in the context of a bigger black hole in the council's finances. The city had received a double whammy during the Thatcher era. The region's traditional industries, shipbuilding and heavy engineering, were abandoned and areas such as Tyneside that were dependent on them were not given the support they needed to restructure. As people consequently left the region, council revenues fell – directly, as a result of fewer people paying council tax, and indirectly, because central government grants are linked to the size of the population. Councils were also legally restricted in their spending and borrowing. The pressure on all council managers, then, was to save money. 'It was a pressure which would have us think short term and lose the wider picture,' says Fred Stephen.

## Responsibility for change

Despite this financial pressure, some people, especially those close to the delivery of the IT services, did keep the wider picture in focus. 'A lot of people were really open to change,' commented Lorraine Dixon, who is now head of ICT services for schools and children's services, reinforcing the recurring message of frustrated aspiration that was beginning to come from every level of the organisation. As manager of IT support services for schools, she had an unusual degree of autonomy at that time and began an impressive process of internal change that made IT services much more responsive to the particular needs of each school than any of the packages she first investigated from the private sector. Her experience was an early example of what could be achieved by public sector managers and staff, building on the relationships and trust that already existed in the council. 'There are a lot of skilled and committed people,' she added.

The fundamental problem was who could lead the process of change, activate this commitment and release these skills. It was the existing management methods which had led to the current impasse without any challenge from the council's leadership. Those who could see the need for change and had a sense of what needed to be done were all too often held back or buried by the directorate hierarchies. A change of direction had to be catalysed from somewhere beyond the existing management.

For many, the virtue of turning to a partnership led by a private company was simply that the private company was bringing in expertise and energy from outside. Surely this would shake things up, so the thinking went.

Of course, such an abdication of responsibility ignores the fact that as far as the public is concerned it is still the council that is in charge – and that is where the buck stops and in reality the risk lands. In Newcastle, moreover, there was one group that wasn't prepared simply to throw the problem over the wall: the unions. Rather than refusing to take responsibility, or merely setting themselves up as defenders of the, short-term interests of staff, the unions instead grasped the nettle of change, understanding their members long term interest lay in making sure that change was public change with strong trade union involvement. They took on responsibility for seeking out an alternative to outsourcing and privatisation, giving encouragement to the managers who wanted to see a process of internal change and creating a political dynamic that attracted others to go along with it.

# Chapter 2

## 'The status quo is not an option'

### What do you mean by 'modernisation' ?

In the face of the problems confronting Newcastle's IT-related services, just about everyone – management, unions and politicians – knew that things had to change. But there was no agreement about the means of change, or the meaning of 'modernisation'. Two contrasting responses to the problem were on offer.

On the one hand Kevin Lavery, Newcastle's new chief executive at the time, was adamant that outsourcing in some form was the much-needed catalyst that would m 'awaken the sleeping giant', thereby changing the organisation and shaking up the culture of the council. The situation was so bad and belief in the capacity of the council to bring about change itself so low that senior management, reluctantly in some cases, saw it as the only solution. Fred Stephen, deputy director of IT at the time, remembers how 'there was a lot to do and it was felt that the best way to achieve the savings would be to engage with the private sector. A range of options was possible, including total outsourcing and the joint venture approach. The early preference was for the latter.'

A joint venture would have meant a private partner in the driving seat and taking a percentage of any savings as profit, with the council holding a minority stake and continuing to take public responsibility. Council employees – those that remained after any restructuring – would have been seconded to the private company under employment conditions that would have been protected for two years.

On the other hand, there was the UNISON branch and, working closely with it on research and advice, the Centre for Public Services an organisation that did research for public sector trade unions and community organisations. They were strongly opposed to any relationship with the private sector that took control over services away from the council. Their key concerns were 'democracy' within Newcastle City Council – and what losing control of public services would mean to that – rather than a generalised hostility to the private sector. On these questions of democracy, so central to the provision of public goods as distinct from commodities for the market, a joint venture was little different from outsourcing. Either way, the council would lose effective control over a key part of its infrastructure and the people of Newcastle would lose the possibility of democratic influence over that infrastructure and its potential benefits. No one was saying that the existing arrangements gave people genuine democratic control but at least the formal power of elected politicians provided a basis and legitimacy for working towards stronger forms of democracy, a basis that would be undermined if management was handed over to a private company.

UNISON and several senior managers also argued that a joint venture would not achieve the necessary savings and improvements in services. A part of any savings would be taken away from the council in the form of profits paid to the private contractor, and many other potential savings would be lost in the fragmentation of 'back office' and 'front office' services that outsourcing would involve. The position of staff would be insecure and lacking the public service motivation that led them to work for the council in the first place.

In August 2000, therefore, Kenny Bell wrote as secretary of the Newcastle council UNISON branch to the council chief executive Kevin Lavery announcing UNISON's opposition to outsourcing.

## Jobs but service improvement too

The trade unions were clear from the beginning that this was not simply about jobs. It was also about the future of public services and the importance of the council's IT capabilities in the development of these services.

For many of the staff active in the campaign to keep Newcastle's IT services in-house, it was also their own competence that was in question. Tony Carr, who was later seconded from his job as a senior administrator on the payroll IT system to be the full-time trade union rep during the process of transformation, saw the motives behind the union campaign like this: 'It's not about resistance to change, it's about controlling your own destiny and not having somebody else come in and manage us through the change. We were saying to the council: "Give us the chance to do it. You're prepared to pay them an awful lot of money on it – are you saying that we aren't capable or competent?"'

## Lessons learned under Thatcherism

UNISON's active commitment to improving services and its self-confidence in its members' ability to make it happen has a history. It is a tradition that has its roots in the early 1980s. In those years, tenants' organisations in the West End of Newcastle began to work together with the trade unionists who repaired their houses, collected their waste, maintained their green spaces, took care of their street lighting and cleaned their streets, to protect these services from privatisation.

The threat at that time came from the Thatcher government's compulsory competitive tendering (CCT) legislation. This required councils to put all their physical services out to tender, to be picked up by the lowest bidder. This would almost certainly have led to a deterioration in services to the city's tenants and in the pay and working conditions of the staff of the City Works department.

Kenny Bell, who worked then as a community organiser in the West End Resource Centre, remembers this collaboration with the unions and how together they won the support of the council for a strategy that effectively subverted CCT. 'We developed a whole strategy, based on improving services,' he says, recalling how closely he worked, in particular, with Tony Atkinson, the highly committed public service manager of City Works, and his young assistant director, Barry Rowland – later to be a key player in the City Service story. 'We were trying to argue that it wasn't all about cost but about broader issues of meeting standards of service and then building these into the specification of the tender. If it was just about cost we'd have lost to the private sector', says Kenny Bell.

In effect, what unions, City Works' management and tenants groups did in the 1980s was to prepare 'in-house bids' to pitch against private competitors. Every physical service provided by the council was kept in-house and under council control on the basis of the improvement plans that were at the core of these 'in-house bids' and which, Rowland now proudly states, 'did achieve a real modernisation in environmental services'.

It was an important precedent, then, and one that meant that when the unions were faced with the council's IT services being put on to the market, they had considerable know-how about how to engage with the procurement process and work with management to construct a serious in-house bid.

## Trades unionists as visionaries

As we shall see, the memories and lessons from this local experience of keeping services in-house whilst improving them at the same time influenced the trade union response to the challenges of the 21st century. Another, national trade union experience of the 1980s with a strong Tyneside presence also lingered at the back of Kenny Bell's mind, at least. This was the experience of 'workers' plans' – a short-lived and all too easily forgotten period when many well-organised shop stewards' committees in manufacturing resisted corporate 'rationalisation', and the closures and redundancies they brought with them, with alternative plans for new products and new ways of organising production.

The 'alternative corporate plan for socially useful production' drawn up in 1975 by the multi-union, multi-skilled shop stewards combine committee in Lucas Aerospace – the aerospace section of Lucas Industries – was the best known. But shop stewards at Vickers, the tank and heavy engineering company with plants along the West End of the Tyne as it wove through the neighbourhoods of Elswick and Scotswood, also drew up a similar plan to save their jobs and their communities.[1] These were inspiring and influential experiences of a strategic trade unionism that had a new relevance in the 21st century for the struggle over the future of public services.

These kinds of innovative and risky strategies from the late 1970s initiated locally and nationally by well-organised shop stewards' committees, went far beyond the traditional defensive role of trade unions. They depended for their success on members at every level contributing their knowledge of their own work, including their knowledge of users' needs and problems. The memories of these experiences reinforced the local council experiences of the 1980s, and had a potent influence especially on Kenny Bell and Dexter Whitfield from the Centre for Public Services.

A central lesson from both experiences, already part of the reflexes of the UNISON branch, was that the first step in any campaign must be to fully involve the members. And this must be a matter not simply of informing and representing them but actively engaging them in

37

researching and defining the problem, developing the strategy and taking action. It also required members in one department being ready to support groups of workers in related departments to defend the common necessity of keeping services public. Both elements of the strategy in turn required a high degree of organisation and a well-informed, confident membership.

### 'It matters that it's a public service that our members work for'

Newcastle's UNISON branch is well resourced and staffed for this task. With 7,300 members out of a totalt workforce of 11,500 it is one of the largest in the region. The council is well unionised (the majority being in UNISON; the GMB is the other main union). Membership fees enable the branch to spend around £220,000 a year on its office and campaigns, research and training. On education and training it also gets strong backing from the union's northern regional office.

It is only possible to work in the union office on the Civic's first floor, if you keep up with the pace of constant organising, arguing – and laughing. With three secretaries (paid by the branch), five full-time elected officers (seconded from jobs with the council) and usually another six or so organisers seconded from the council for specific jobs, all working in one medium size room, the atmosphere is purposeful but noisy and hectic.

There is a strongly shared culture here. It is evident in the attitude shown to the union members. The branch organisers grumble about the members on occasion but they share a general respect for their knowledge of their jobs and their commitment as public servants to improving the services they provide. Josie Bird, recently elected chair of the UNISON branch, explains its traditions: 'We recognise that our members choose to work in the public sector ... in many cases they could get much better money elsewhere.'

There is also a shared belief in the importance of developing the unions' bargaining power to work to defend and improve services, as well as to look after members' pay and working conditions. The collaboration as equals with management to improve services has always been based on the union's autonomy and industrial strength. The unions' ability to escalate an issue, even to the point of strike action, is as important to this story as the managers' ability to manage.

A striking feature of the early part of the story of the City Service transformation is the way that the staff's confidence in their ability to be drivers of change grew the deeper they went into the bidding process, the more they found out about the private competitors, the more they discovered their own collective capacity and potential. This growth in the confidence and strategic know-how of a core of staff who were active in the campaign to keep the service in-house turned out to be a largely hidden influence – but vital for nourishing the transformation process itself. But we are running ahead of ourselves.

When UNISON officials first heard of the plans for a joint venture in August 2000 they organised meetings of all the members across the ITRS department (most of the staff were in UNISON, managers at all levels included). 'From very early on, as soon as there was news of market testing, we had to go out and get them to recruit reps from each group. It's a basic principle: if workers are facing a problem, then hold a mass meeting and get reps elected or volunteered. From early on we had a ITRS rep for every section,' reports Kenny Bell. From this moment until the completion of the basic transformation process, there was a group of up to 35 trade union representatives from all the ITRS sections meeting initially every fort-night, sometimes every week and then every month or so across what became City Service. From the standpoint of understanding the changes that were needed to improve the IT and related services, the unions had an advantage on management, which still worked in silos, often with little communication across departments.

## Three steps to public service heaven ...
### Step 1: Opening the procurement process
The ITRS trade union working group made it their first priority to establish a visible presence within the council's 'procurement process' (that is, the way the council put a service 'out to tender' to attract bids from the market and then the way that it assessed those bids and decided which to accept) as soon as possible. This meant that the first public announcement by the council of the proposed joint venture (the 'OJEC notice') also had to make clear that there would be an in-house bid. The trade union working group also participated in determining the evaluation

criteria for the bidders, insisting on trade union access, under commercial confidentiality, to all bids, and direct contact with the bidders.

Since the trade unions' ultimate purpose was to achieve a serious council proposal to transform the IT services, a strong motive behind accessing the procurement process was to monitor progress – or, as it turned out in the first few months, lack of it – on the in-house bid. They needed to be ready to exert pressure at every point, in order to be taken seriously. (There is a procedure in local government of having a formal 'comparator', which is sometimes presented as an in-house bid but is in fact little more than a description of the status quo of the existing 'business' as carried out by the council and is used as the lowest bench mark on which the private sector bidder has to improve.)

The group of people  trade union reps – who took time off from their normal work to press for an in-house bid were intervening in a process with which few trade unions have previously engaged – and over which management generally assumed they had a prerogative that was not open to negotiation. Indeed, the procurement process doesn't sound like the normal stuff of trade union activism. Kenny Bell explains its importance: 'Our aim at this first stage was to get an in-house bid taken seriously. When management said, 'We are looking at this' (meaning the 'in-house bid'), we knew that they were looking at a baseline of how services are provided now compared to how the private sector could provide them. That would mean inevitably that the private sector bid would win. We had to recognise that even though we were against the whole concept of market testing, if we actually wanted to win an in-house bid we had to intervene at that level from the start.'

Things were moving fast. In December 2000, the OJEC notice was published with the trade union amendments. Thirty companies responded with formal expressions of interest. By August 2001, these had boiled down to three: CSL, British Telecom and Unisys. Back on the first floor of the Civic, where the chief executive had his office, however, there was no sign that the in-house bid was being worked on as a serious option rather than a base comparator. UNISON kept up constant pressure. In March 2001, Kenny Bell wrote complaining that the management was giving no leadership on the in-house bid; in July 2001, he requested a meeting with senior management to clarify the timetable for the in-house bid; and so on.

### Step 2: Making democracy matter

The UNISON reps knew that traditional forms of trade union pressure would not be sufficient on their own to secure an in-house bid. They were to take industrial action, as we shall see; it was vital in showing the strength of staff feeling about keeping services public – and, incidentally, giving at least one would-be bidder a glimpse of what industrial relations might be like if the joint venture went ahead. But this industrial action was part of a far wider political campaign aimed at raising the awareness of the consequences of privatisation winning the backing of councillors against any form of privatisation and for a serious in-house plan for change.

So the second strategic focus was on the elected politicians. Kenny Bell again explains: 'The political pressure was key. We had to open up the debate. That meant engaging with the political process, which ultimately decides the direction of the local authority.'

This focus on the elected politicians was also a matter of democracy. The unions no more wanted to take the final decisions about who should deliver services than they wanted management to take them. Newcastle was known as an 'officer-led' local council. The local UNISON branch's vision was not to substitute union officials for council officers but to make sure that the council was genuinely 'democracy-led'.

A small band of councillors shared the union's opposition to privatisation; the campaign's objective was to help them win the argument with the rest of the Labour group. (Until 2004, Newcastle was Labour controlled; the Lib-Dems then won control.) 'We were also aiming to spread awareness and build up political pressure from our membership and the broader public,' adds Kenny Bell.

Most council staff are also Newcastle residents and the local UNISON is proud of its engagement with the politics of the city, from defending and improving public services generally to counteracting the influence of the BNP. Throughout the campaign, the branch was very media savvy, always bearing in mind different ways of explaining the case against privatisation and for public-led change. 'There's no way that trade union activity by itself could have stopped the steamroller. We needed to reach out and win allies,' says John Field, the UNISON branch's press officer at the time.

### Step 3: Analysis, arguments and alternatives

To be effective on these two fronts of engagement required analysis, arguments and alternatives. So this was the third category of items that UNISON's ITRS meetings would discuss.

The branch had developed a distinctively participatory approach to research and developing alternatives. It regularly employed Dexter Whitfield from the Centre for Public Services to prepare reports. The list is impressive, from *Outsourcing the Future: A Social and Economic Audit of Privatisation Proposals in Newcastle*,[2] through detailed reports on the experience of joint ventures and privatisation elsewhere to a detailed investigation of the record of BT (who eventually became the sole outside bidder). Whitfield worked with the shop stewards to collate and follow up their insights, analysis and questions. For example, when BT delivered its bid, 15 reps crowded into the central Newcastle offices that the company was using and spent the day with Dexter assessing the document.

For UNISON shop steward and housing benefits worker Lisa Marshall, it was a turning point: 'I realised then that private business did not have any special expertise. As we looked over their bid with Dexter, we found a lot that we knew could be done better. From then on I felt confident about what we were trying to do keeping it in-house.'

A collaborative approach to research, which built confidence and strategic thinking, therefore, bore fruit not only in the campaign for the in house bid but in the process of transformation itself through building the self-confidence and wider perspective of the staff.

## Our city is not for sale

The branch decided it had to apply this strategy across the council's services. Chief executive Kevin Lavery's outsourcing plans were council-wide. The branch leadership knew they could not halt the drive to outsource service by service. 'We realised we had to run a generalised campaign, raising awareness of the extent of the privatisation and what its consequences would be,' says Kenny Bell.

This campaign combined well-researched analysis and presentation of alternatives with strike action initially spearheaded by those workers affected by the numerous plans for outsourcing or other forms of privatisation. Strike action was an important tactic to highlight the urgency of the issue and draw attention to the union's argument. The first proposed strike was on 10 February 2001 and involved UNISON members only – 50 anti-privatisation housing staff voted to walk out. As a result of UNISON's efforts to 'raise awareness of the wider consequences' of privatisation, however, thousands of other members also took action in support of them.

The branch then began to work towards a more ambitious day of strike action seven months later supported by all groups of workers, whether or not they were directly affected by privatisation, and by all the council unions – the GMB, the building workers, UCATT, the engineering workers, Amicus, and the TGWU. The press, in particular the *Newcastle Evening Chronicle*, were sympathetic too. Another channel for broadening support came with the creation of a Public Services Alliance by community, trade union and political organisations that shared a commitment to defending and improving public services. This included Don Price and five other Labour councillors who in early 2001 faced disciplinary action and threats of expulsion from the Labour Group for opposing privatisation.[3]

Despite the strength of support, the day of strike action did not go smoothly. The night before the strike, the council obtained an injunction declaring it illegal under the Thatcher government's unrepealed legislation against unions taking supportive action. But as John Field, branch publicity officer, remembers: 'On the day, thousands of members stayed away from work and lots of people turned up saying, "Hang on, some of my colleagues/mates are not in work, I'm not prepared to come in," and left.' What's more, adds Field, 'There was a massive public outcry in the local press about the council using anti-trade union laws.'

## Political turnaround

Even though the day of action did not go according to plan, it had a dramatic effect on the future of the ITRS. A week later, one of the private bidder CSL withdrew, publicly citing UNISON's opposition to its staff transfer plans as the main reason. Three weeks later, a number of resolutions on the future of public services came before the Labour group. The council's final decision on the improvement of services reads as follows: 'Our aim is to achieve this (the improvement of services) through improved in-house services not privatisation ...'

The crucial commitment for the future of the council's IT services was this: that the council would use alternatives to in-house provision only if 'a full in-house' option had been prepared and 'there are still significant improvements to the service which cannot be achieved in-house'. The resolution concluded: 'Group further agrees to support a campaign to persuade government to move away from the privatisation agenda.' The resolution was passed overwhelmingly.

The political turnaround was both dramatic and impressive.

One factor was undoubtedly the cumulative evidence of private sector inefficiency, especially after the first year or two of a contract. This came from well-publicised national calamities such as the collapse of privatised housing benefit systems in London and the personal experiences of councillors in their everyday jobs.

Don Price, at that time a councillor in the East End of the city, for example, is a building inspector. The government's building control service had been outsourced under the Thatcher governments. 'The standard has plummeted,' he told me, adding: 'My experience was quite common to councillors who had found that the promise of efficiencies and savings from privatisation had proved to be an illusion.' Several senior managers also described how colleagues' similar experiences of outsourcing strategic services had influenced their growing scepticism about the joint venture.

Another important factor was that the core of councillors strongly committed in principle against privatisation were able to convince wavering colleagues by using information from regular meetings with UNISON. 'Decisions at that time were taken on the basis of Powerpoint presentations, without written reports. The information from the unions was crucial; telling us what was really going on,' says Don Price.

Another factor was the pressure of voters, influenced by the UNISON campaign and the sympathetic projection it got from the press. This was crucial in winning over a middle group of councillors, normally loyal to the leadership but with traditional Labour loyalties.

This conversion of the Labour Group was fundamental to the success of the campaign for the in-house bid. It gave political legitimacy to UNISON's arguments for in-house provision, and it gave backbone to managers committed to keeping public services public.

## A new balance of forces

By the end of 2001, a very different balance of forces and emerging possibilities had developed in the corridors of the Civic. BT was by now the only private bidder. It had become the 'preferred' bidder and was given a room on the first floor to draw up its bid with full access to all the council information that it needed.

But down the corridor, the office of chief executive was empty. Kevin Lavery had left to join Jarvis plc. By this time his political support had evaporated. Now the possibility – not yet the reality – of an in house-bid was beginning to be taken seriously by a minority of senior managers. BT however, did not take seriously, it seemed to some of those working with the BT team, the possibility of competition from within the council. Faced with this situation the UNISON ITRS Working Group adopted a 'twin track' strategy of scrutinising BT's proposals while sharing knowledge and skills across IT services in order to be clear about the alternatives and ready to contribute to the in-house with relevant options.

As far as the in-house bid was concerned, the union was always clear that it was management that must finally pull it together. 'We never considered drawing up our own proposal for an in-house bid, mainly because if management didn't "own" it, it would not succeed,' says Ian Farrell, a rep from Revenues. The ITRS union reps developed clear ideas themselves, though, about what any such bid should contain.

Meanwhile, what management began to hear about BT's proposals led them to take the in-house proposal seriously. As Fred Stephens told us, 'The profits BT had to take out of their deal in order to satisfy their shareholders made theirs a very unattractive proposition.' He went on to explain: 'I am not ideologically opposed to engaging the private sector, but what BT proposed was simply a bad deal for the council and its taxpayers.'

Senior management, most notably Barry Rowland, who in the vacuum left by the departure of Kevin Lavery was the decisive figure, also came to recognise that a crucial factor in favour of the in-house bid was the commitment of the staff to making it work.

Everyone concerned would agree that, in the words of Don Price, then (in 2001) Labour deputy leader of the council, 'Barry was key.' As we have seen, Kevin Lavery had been the driver of the procurement process as chief executive but Barry Rowland, who at that time bore the hopeful title of director of strategic change, had considerable power in the council.

Initially Rowland, a pragmatic and cautious man, had been very doubtful about an in-house process of change. He had little faith in the existing management of IT services to lead such a process, however competent they were in managing the existing system. There was no IT equivalent of the City Works manager Tony Atkinson who led improvements in the 1970s. A lot more was at stake than in the kind of contracts for which he and the unions had prepared in City Works: the successful bidder for the ITRS joint venture stood to win an 11-year, £250 million contract.

## An alternative in the making

An important step in the development of staff involvement was a series of workshops on the bid in May 2002 – one for management, one for staff and a final joint workshop, which asked 'Why are we in this position?', 'Do we have the capability and willingness to change?' and 'What would happen if we did not change?', and went on to agree guiding principles for the in-house option. Staff made sure the workshops were not a one-off but were followed by informal staff input into the detail of change, regular meetings of ITRS reps and meetings with leading councillors. 'We were insistent on this political involvement, even if it meant being chaperoned by management,' says Tony Carr, (later seconded to be a full time trade union representative for all those in the IT related services). The union learnt to be insistent on joint mechanisms for every aspect of the process.

The workshops revealed perspectives distinct to management and staff. 'We stressed the need for integration between departments and between back office and customer services,' said one trade union rep. 'We see things service-wide because that is how we are organised, it's where our strength is. Management tend to have a much more departmental view.'

There was more caution from staff than management about over-reliance on new technology. Take Lisa Marshall and Jean Dunlop, working on housing benefits and debt collection respectively. They are 'back-office' workers, employed to discuss problems with people on the phone. As Jean Dunlop put it: 'It's about retaining control in order to be able to follow things through with someone, build a rapport.' According to Lisa Marshall, 'We get a lot of people from vulnerable groups or with problems of literacy. You just can't get away from people's feeling that they want to deal with a person. There was talk of getting rid of direct access and creating portals so people just keyed in their details. Any new system must involve the option of direct personal contact.'

Newcastle ITRS workers wanted to use the new technology to improve communication and make services more responsive to users with all their variety of needs. Staff felt they understood the needs of the public in a way a private company could not, and that this was a strong reason for keeping IT services within the council.

In the past the 'back office' and 'front-of-house' services had been linked, but the automation of back office work plus an increasing emphasis on the public image of the council could, the staff feared, sharpen the distinction. From what the Newcastle reps could see, BT's approach would widen this gap. 'We went to Liverpool [where BT already had a joint venture with the council] and the front of house was all very glossy and people seemed happy with the changes; it was from the back that the grumbling came. We didn't want to be second-class citizens,' says Tony Carr.

Although it had not been their intention, the workshops effectively challenged much of the arguments for outsourcing as the apparent answer to the council's problems with its IT system and services. They fortified the council workers' confidence to challenge BT's selling points. BT, for instance, claimed a management free to 'take hard decisions'. Council workers replied that if they meant they would 'take on' the unions that would rebound on the council and be expensive and counter-productive. The in-house option aimed to work more efficiently with the unions, negotiating commitments to training or redeployment and avoiding compulsory redundancies. These assurances were important because they meant staff were more likely to feel secure enough to take on change.

Again, where BT stressed its capacity to provide economies of scale, the staff workshops responded that 'with in-house change we can form partnerships with other public bodies.' BT suggested its involvement would be good for the city's image, perhaps attracting further investment. The staff countered that an efficient, publicly-run IT service could achieve the same by building up genuine confidence in the council's own abilities – even broadening the scope of the public sector to develop the regional economy.

Some truths were told on all sides during these half-day discussions. Outside the context of the normal hierarchies, both management and staff were able to drop some defences and acknowledge room for improvement.

The final joint workshop tested and built up commitment to the in-house bid, based on the principle reiterated again and again by the union leadership that 'the status quo is not an option'. Their determined rejection of the joint venture with a private company was matched by an equally strong insistence that the way the services were presently managed and organised would have to change.

It was not simply a matter of introducing the new technology. Kenny Bell was insistent on this: 'A lot of the blocks to change that we identified at those workshops were about management culture and the way managers were used to manage. The idea of culture change and transforming the way the services were organised became a key part of the in-house bid.'

## A hard days night: writing the in-house bid

On the management side, disappointment with the BT bid, together with a recognition that the unions were, on certain conditions, committed to real change, finally led, at the last minute, to a serious in-house bid. Three senior managers put it together in around three weeks. According to Fred Stephen, 'We put in unprecedented hours – 80 hours a week – and I remember sitting propped up in bed at midnight proof-reading. When the document came together, it showed that if it could be made to work the council would be achieving far greater levels of savings than with BT – more than double in fact.'

The anticipated job losses were fewer than BT's, but at 153 full-time equivalents (out of a workforce of 650) still considerable. To some extent these 153 jobs were a currency, measured in terms of a 'D' grade post, which is worth around £20,000, and a significant number of jobs were at a senior level. But all levels that were cut were affected and redeployment and retraining was a central part of the transformation process, as we shall see.

In September 2002, the council accepted the in-house option. This was at a time when the government was promoting joint venture or strategic service partnerships of exactly the kind that Kevin Lavery had hoped Newcastle would pioneer. Instead, the council decided to pioneer a public approach to the transformation of a strategic service. It has proved to be an important precedent, demonstrating that putting a strategic service out to tender need not lead to private control.

The language here is so inert and stodgy – 'in-house bids', 'procurement processes', 'strategic delivery services' – that it is difficult to convey the importance of what has happened. It is worth emphasising: people's commitment to carrying out a public service, with co-operation between departments and between management and staff, has been recognised as able to deliver a public service *more efficiently* than a company working for profit. The foundations were laid by a model born out of a struggle in which staff and managers believed it *mattered* who owned and controlled the service for reasons of genuine efficiency in responding to the needs and desires of the public, which in a public service is closely connected to democracy.

The in-house bid achieved its purpose, clinching the argument for a public leadership of the process of transformation and improvement. It consisted of a self-financing model delivering gross revenue savings of £34.5 million (£28 million net savings ) over eleven and a half years to support frontline services in need of investment. Savings would start in year one (2003/4). It involved £20 million investment in new systems, refreshing existing systems and implementing the changes.

But how far did the bid provide an adequate compass for steering the transformation in practice? And did the practice live up to the vision of the campaign? This is best judged through the experience of those who were given or took responsibility personally to lead the change.

1. See Huw Benyon and Hilary Wainwright, *The Workers Report on Vickers Ltd*, Pluto Press 1980
2. http://www.european-services-strategy.org.uk/outsourcing-library/public-costs/outsourcing-the-future-a-social-and-economic-a/
3. 'The Labour whip proposed expulsion from the Labour Group and it was discussed first at the executive and then at the Labour Group. The Labour Group decided against the expulsion.

# Chapter 3

## Making it happen

### The team: some introductions

One of the things clearly to emerge from the staff and management workshops in the build up to the in-house bid was the need for a strong team to drive the required change. Kenny Bell, Tony Carr, Lisa Marshall and others in the UNISON ITRS/City Service group would be the first to say that others were crucial in keeping Newcastle's IT services public. They would point, in particular, to the rebel councillors with whom they worked to build up majority political support for the in-house option, and to Barry Rowland and Fred Stephen, the senior managers who eventually put their weight behind the in-house bid.

Everyone was necessary; no one alone was sufficient – and it is a distinctive feature of this story that there is no macho-style claiming of ownership. Even so, it is clear that it was these union activists who lost sleep over the effort to ensure that there was an effective in-house bid. From early 2003 onwards, though, it was the turn of a group of managers to drive forward the process of change. Though union reps continued to lose sleep too!

### A new spirit of public sector management

The council's management team for City Service come from a variety of backgrounds, mostly public sector but some private, and from a range of generations, the youngest in her thirties, the oldest in his fifties. Interestingly, perhaps, the majority are women. What they have in common is an energetic determination to bring about change the public way, with a strong commitment to the importance of genuinely involving the staff at every stage and an ability to learn pragmatically from experiences in the private sector. The biographies of some of the key people offer a sense of the team.

## Ray Ward

Meeting challenges and fixing problems has been the common theme of Ray Ward's employment history. He's the man the council appointed as head of City Service. His first job in local government, in the finance department at Leeds City Council, aged 16, gave him an inside experience of what needed to change. He had chosen local government as the 'best place to sleep' as he recovered from nightly gigs playing the guitar and singing in a rock group. Many of his managers seemed to be sleeping too. He developed the 'icing sugar test', dusting his managers' desks with icing sugar to see if anything moved. Mostly it didn't.

Once he realised that his passion for music wasn't going to pay the mortgage, he began a career in local government. From Richmond through Plymouth, Hereford and finally the East Riding, he left no chance for the icing sugar to settle. But he didn't entirely leave the spirit of his days as a musician behind.

'I don't like work,' he says, speaking about releasing the creativity that he believes exists in everyone. 'I prefer playing, having fun. If we need to be serious, we will be serious – when I'm standing in committee [meetings] I haven't got a red nose on – and you've got to be professional when you need to be professional. But let's not get carried away with it. Make work fun. Remove the sense of fear, of blame; remove the constraints to thinking, doing and acting ...'

The liberation of people's creativity has been a consistent theme running through the management practice of City Service. Ray Ward insisted that recruitment adverts for the rest of the team after his appointment should reach out to people who felt their creativity had been stifled. 'Are you frustrated?' asked the final – and effective – job ads. Traditional local government advertisements had gone out previously for a 'chief executive for exchequer services'. But as Ray Ward puts it, 'Who dreams of being chief exec of exchequer services when they grow up?' and not surprisingly the first crop of candidates was unlikely to meet the challenge of the new City Service.

## Kath Moore

Kath Moore exudes a calm confidence in the capacity of the public sector to reform itself at the same time as being fully aware of the obstacles. She has the 'nous' of an insider (she's worked for the council for more than 15 years) but has somehow managed to retain the mentality of an iconoclast who has no fear of change as long as it's driven by values she shares. 'My core belief,' she says, 'is that the public sector can be as good as – and in some ways better than – the private sector [in the management of public services] because of its social values.

Kath Moore was Ray Ward's first appointment, to lead the Business, Development and Transformation team. This team, was, in effect, a special team of diplomats and drivers of change. It was both autonomous from and collaborated closely with the different sections of City Service responsible for day-to-day service provision.

Kath had been working with cooks, cleaners, caretakers and others who provide the day-to-day services for Newcastle schools on how to improve those services. She had shown how improvements could be achieved by listening to the cooks and cleaners who provided the services. 'They had so many ideas and solutions' she said, 'mainly because they really understood and listened to their service users'.

The roots of her belief, she explains 'is founded on the people who work in the public sector. There is so much talent, commitment, energy and passion to get it right for our service users,' she says that 'any organisation with that potential, must, given the right leadership, go on to great success'. She determined that, as far she was concerned, 'We shouldn't be mimicking the private sector. We must be ourselves. We must find ways of being innovative on our own terms, and in closer partnership with our service users.'

This commitment leads her to apply the methodology of 'business' to the public sector and meeting social goals. She doesn't mean private business in particular in this context, she says, but simply the general principle of thinking rigorously about the best ways of allocating limited resources to meet specified goals. 'We should always be trying to find the best way of using taxpayers' money to meet social goals – that's what business means to me,' she says, 'and doing it in an organised, transparent way.'

For Moore, good organisation means 'engaging people in the change, listening to people doing the job, knowing that they are full of good ideas, ensuring that we show people how valued they are and appreciated'. That was the lesson she learnt from her schools' experience – through, for example, doing things like creating 'an annual cooks' conference where all of the cooks came in for a day. We put a lot of effort into organising it as a conference that would make a real difference. It had quite a buzz about it.' When she heard about the job with City Service, she savoured the idea of doing similar work, creating a buzz on a much bigger scale.

## Steve Evans

Steve Evans was the next catch from the trawl of managers looking for a challenge. He was attracted by the recruitment advertisement's appeal for someone 'working in an organisation that is struggling to grasp that transformational rather than incremental change is the only way forward ... and with change and people-skills that mean you see things other managers can't'. He says he has always been eager to move on when things become repetitive. He left a previous post at Sainsbury's because of the 'limits of being in an organisation where there's one way of doing things and it is dictated from on high'. He moved on to set up a customer service centre for Herefordshire Council. In 2003 he was looking for bigger opportunities than a council the size of Herefordshire could offer.

When Steve Evans arrived in Newcastle he faced the public sector equivalent of the uniformity and dictat from above that he'd found in Sainsbury's. He looked askance at the 'one size fits all, check list box approach' that the council employed to solve the difficulties of delivering a wide and increasingly complex set of services. His belief was that 'solutions have to be service-specific and respond to people's actual needs'. In his new job he was pleased to have the authority to change fundamentally the way things were done, including management structures, to give autonomy to people closer to the frontline delivery of services.

An open, friendly and straightforward man, Steve could often be found, as the transformation progressed, striding cheerfully between his different responsibilities as manager of exchequer services in the 'Civic' and the person with overall responsibility for 'revs and bens' (revenues and benefits) in the tatty Scottish Life House building five minutes down the road. (By the time this book was finished he had delegated most of his management responsibilities for revenues and benefits to a new manager.)

Like others in the team, he draws confidently on private sector techniques and radically adapts then to useful public sector goals. Take the provision of information, for example. He describes how shocked he was on arrival at Newcastle at 'the lack of management information, financial information, budgetary information, volume information ...' It was almost impossible to make informed decisions because 'you didn't have anything to base it on other than gut instinct'.

In the private sector, by contrast, he'd found 'absolute clarity about the key information necessary for running the business'. The private sector has a very simple bottom line, he says: 'If it doesn't add value for the shareholders, don't do it. But there's no reason why this sense of focus can't be applied to an organisation that has the complexity of local government, and where the bottom line is quality of service.' Again, it's not an approach that seeks to mimic the private sector but instead claims and adapts principles of efficiency and value for money for social goals and public institutions.

## Helen Batey

A notably energetic and outward going person, Helen Batey was manager of customer services in the old regime. Her background is housing, where for 22 years as a 'front-line kind of person', she had consulted people on demolition, City Challenge and other regeneration issues. She is a champion of the 'one stop shop' idea of the customer service centre, and more generally the idea of giving the public a unified and convenient service to which they have easy and seamless access. 'The public loved it,' she says, 'but we had to fight with senior and middle management.' She looks exhausted at the memory of it. 'I've been on a management journey for the last five years and it can be very tiring.'

Helen was perhaps the main driver in practical terms of City Service's focus on the public and what they want. She had support at the highest level: first, former Newcastle chief executive Kevin Lavery and then Barry Rowland were willing to challenge managers who didn't get it. Like others in the management team, she has a strong commitment to demonstrating that public services can be provided better and more effectively within the public sector.

She has a restless air, never content with what has been achieved so far and always seeking further improvements. On questions of consultation and involvement, for example, she says, 'We (the council) are a long way off what can be achieved.' In setting up City Service, she ensured that local people weren't just consulted but were kept involved throughout the process to monitor the development of the design and then the workings of each customer service centre. Helen has now been given the job of leading the council's community engagement strategy, to apply lessons from City Service to wider issues of how to engage citizens more fully with the operation of their council.

**Julia Woollard**

Originally, Julia Woollard worked at HSBC. She says 'working in the City was a real buzz, and I learnt loads [but] I was increasingly feeling that there was more to life than shareholder profit'. She answered a job ad for Newcastle Council and became the programme manager of the transformation programme – a kind of anchor, progress chaser and information hub, all in one. Her knowledge of the workings of the private sector was put to good use in her increasingly confident negotiations with Fujitsu, who helped with the process of change, especially in procuring the IT hardware.

Julia is another calm but determined force in the transformation, business and development team. She also shares a strong and pragmatic commitment to the public leadership of the transformation process: 'It makes me shudder to think about how we could be responsive and improve services across the council if we didn't have control of our ICT,' she says. Her priority in dealings with the private sector, beyond a tight control over invoices and prices, is to ensure maximum transfer of knowledge. In this way, the upgrading of public sector skills and confidence grows out of a relationship with the private sector, rather than the public sector being weakened as a result of contracting out tasks – which is so often the result of outsourcing.

## Ron Hillaby

A senior manager in Newcastle's IT section with a

record of 26 years working as an IT analyst for the council, Ron Hillaby is the most modest of men. He only really shows off when he is demonstrating the scope of one of the new IT packages that he and his team have worked on, and even then it is the technology he talks up, not himself.

'It was always understood that there would be a small amount of work on reconfiguration of the programme – nothing that would change how the system actually worked,' he explains. 'There's the core software that runs the system that you don't change because that's the way the system operates. The decision was that the business would adapt to suit the package rather than the other way round, because the package was based on best practice. That's the theory.'

The reality has been more complex – and very demanding of time and other resources. 'For instance,' explains Ron, 'if you look at the revenues and benefits package, there are constant new releases of software. They have to be taken in, they have to be tried out, and then they have to be handed out to the users for testing before you can roll them out live, and there's a lot of work in this.'

He found that far from dealing with the problem of redundancies, his main challenge was to keep people: 'When the transformation programme started, people were saying, "Well, if we're not going to develop systems anymore, what am I going to do? Because that's the nature of my work – I develop systems." Our work would move from actually developing the applications to working on the integration of those applications. I had to do a lot of work with the staff to explain to them how I envisaged them working in this brave new world and how the council would still need those resources.'

Ron, along with the rest of the city service, also had a challenge to get the council to understand how to use information and information technology to improve services: 'In the past it's really been about just feeding information in, which allows the day-to-day operation of the system. What the council sort of struggled to grasp is that information can also be important in service improvement, in making your service more efficient, and just generally keeping managers a bit more informed about the service.' Beneath his reserved demeanour, in his creative understanding of the connection between IT and the improvement of frontline services, Ron has been a key resource along with the rest of the IT team in the transformation process.

## Jeff Pasternack
A distinctive addition to the team of project leaders at the end of 2003 was Jeff Pasternack, an IT manager from New York with experience in both the private and public sectors and an aura of energy and readiness for action. He'd just received a severance package from his previous employer when he saw one of the 'Are you frustrated?' advertisements. It appealed to him. 'It was, you know, pop art – just do it!' he says. 'It had that kind of spirit, which I love.'

When he came to Newcastle for the City Service interviews, he recalls being 'really impressed. I thought they recruited really well.' He was struck too by 'a sense of jocularity, whether from management or the unions. They weren't heavy-handed with us, and there was a sense of "No limits, let's do something."'

# Chapter 4

## The financial means and constraints

It was just as well that the City Service management team were a determined, confident – and humorous – bunch. City Service head Ray Ward describes what he found in his first week on the first floor of the Civic. 'There were a lot of senior people outside City Service who were saying this thing had just been set up to fail, set up to buy time. They said the procurement process hadn't been thought through properly, that [the council had] got themselves into a corner, they needed to save face, they needed an exit. "City Service is their exit, Ray, that's all it is," these people told me, "I know what's behind it; it's not going to work." The failure of City Service was on the council's list of "top ten strategic risks".'

Almost from the first day Ray Ward sat down at his desk, the clock started to tick. There was an imperative to meet savings targets, starting in year one, that seemed to have an air of life and death about it, not least because the threat of outsourcing had not been entirely banished. As we shall see, moreover, the City Service business model was necessarily complex. It was not a matter of making savings per se, which would have been challenging enough, but of making them *through improving the quality of the services* – with these improvements being achieved through concerted *transformation* rather than incremental change.

So how was the City Service process of transformation funded? What was the financial model, and how did it work in practice? How did it achieve sufficient flexibility to achieve the brief that elected politicians had finally agreed? How did it cope with a changing environment – in terms of technology, politics and strategic priorities?

The brief, to recap on the principles of the in-house bid, was to radically overhaul the technology and the organisation so that services to residents and to the rest of the council were improved, enabling staff to give of their best, while making major back-office savings to re-allocate to frontline services, both in City Service and across the council as a whole.

## Financial storm clouds and sunshine

The council treasurer, Paul Woods, is the man best equipped to explain. His demeanour is friendly but serious. He joined the council as a young trainee, making his way from tea-boy to treasurer and carries a strong sense of being a public servant, a custodian of the taxpayers' interests – and not just because of his position as the person with ultimate legal responsibility for the council's finances. A dramatic picture of the Tyne Bridge with the sun breaking through a gathering storm greets you as you enter his room. He says it reminded him of the Newcastle Council treasurer's department: 'storm clouds all round, the treasury breaking through'.

City Service certainly needed a share of the sun. The storm clouds also affected the whole of the council. Paul

Woods explains the context in measured terms: 'Ever since the first rate capping in 1994 we have been under pressure to look for savings.' At the time of the transformation, the council had to find savings of £4-6 milion per annum. 'Ever since then, government grants to the council had been below the rate of inflation, and we face added cost pressures as a result of the cost of ensuring equal pay for women and men, having more older people to care for and more young people with special needs.'

'Since the early 1990s, the pressure has been to reduce costs and to improve quality,' he adds. 'Now [2008] the requirement is to drive 3 per cent efficiency savings out of the system each year and there is a massive pressure on affordability' with the local commitment to keep the increase in council tax to the rate of inflation or less while protecting frontline services. The 2008/09 savings target was £13 million and the 2009/10 target is £20 million.

To finance its initial investment in the transformation process, City Service was able to benefit from Gordon Brown's 2004 prudential borrowing scheme. Brown's scheme lets councils borrow money to be repaid out of future income or savings. So Newcastle could borrow £20 million to implement the plan laid out in the in-house bid. Over an 11½-year period, £13 million was to be spent on 'technical refresh' (replacing all the council's servers and computers on a rolling cycle) and £7 million on new systems and implementation.

The model was self-financing. The transformation itself was projected to take just four years (2003-2007) and to deliver a total of £34.5 million in gross savings (£28 million in net savings after redundancy and contingency costs) over the 11½ years. The loan would be repaid over the same period. As changes were introduced – new applications, new technology management systems, the new organisational structures – savings would be made, and the loan begun to be paid back. The earlier that savings were made, the greater the overall benefit.

The in-house model delivers significantly higher levels of savings to the council than the outsourcing proposal would have provided. Indeed, over the 11½-year period, the transformation programme only needed to deliver 33 per cent of its projected savings to secure an improved financial position for the council in its first years. This meant that the management of City Service was able, in negotiation with Paul Woods, to interpret the model flexibly over the timing of the savings so long as, in his words, it was 'moving in the right direction'.

'We did move things around,' says Ray Ward. 'Things do get in the way and on the other hand opportunities present themselves. So the sequence changed, which meant that the investment had to change, which meant that the savings profiles had to change. The main aim was to achieve these high levels of savings and improvement.'

## A crucial relationship
The relationship between City Service and the treasurer was important. He sat in on the steering committee of

the transformation programme throughout and was actively involved from time to time. 'He was the first person I would go to discuss interpretations of the model. He's been involved all the way,' remembers Ray Ward.

A particularly important example of how this crucial relationship worked came during 2005, when it was clear that the savings target for the financial year 2005/06 was not going to be met. The main reason was that the document management system (DMS) implemented in revenues and benefits to handle electronic versions of the millions of council tax, housing benefits and other documents that City Service dealt with wasn't delivering the expected efficiencies. Fujitsu, the outside contractors who had been hired to bring in new hardware and software on a 'guaranteed maximum price' contract, took the responsibility for this shortfall and shouldered the cost of replacing the system with a new one that was more appropriate for Newcastle. Even so, although City Service did not have to bear the cost of buying a new system, its whole savings programme was put out of joint by not having an efficiently functioning system for electronically managing the documents with which most of the staff were working.

Ray Ward had to explain to Paul Woods why City Service was not delivering the half a million pounds worth of savings that should have come from, among other things, introducing the DMS and improving many processes relating to the staff's ability to raise the quality of their work.

Paul Woods agreed to rephase the loan repayments: 'We recognised that it was going to take longer. We did some creative accounting to give them "wiggle room", as Ray calls it.' His reasoning is revealing about the culture and the relationships surrounding City Service: 'Having made the decision [to go with the in-house bid] we supported it, we wanted to make it work. It was a bold decision. In fact we had to make it work. They were going in the right direction.' And, he adds: 'Their style of working helped. There was an honesty. We got round the table and worked it through.'

This whole story is one about the possibilities of publicly-driven public sector change. But throughout, at every decisive moment, it is worth quietly asking the question: 'What if this work had been outsourced?' In this instance, the flexibility and collaboration evident and decisive in the relationship between the leadership of these two departments of one council with shared public service goals would instead have been a relationship between a contractor and a client. Every change would have been a time-consuming process of negotiation involving charges and costs at every point.

## A different way of doing business
It is worth reflecting briefly for a moment on the nature of the City Service business model. In Newcastle there has been an emphasis on the business case at the same time as a strong emphasis on public service values. In the climate created by 30 years of knocking the public sector, the word 'business' has come to evoke the model of a

private company producing for a market. So, using the word in a public service context currently suggests applying private sector or market logic to the delivery of public goods.

This wasn't what was meant by doing good business in Newcastle, however. In fact, the City Service story shows a distinctive business model for the delivery of public services, one based ultimately on political – in theory democratic – decisions about the allocation of tax to meet citizens' basic social needs. It is a model based on the maximisation of public benefit, not profit – subject to the cost saving constraints mentioned above, which were built into the self-financing of the transformation.

Kath Moore puts it well when she says: 'We should always be trying to find the best way of using taxpayers' money to meet social goals – that's what business means to me. We should never take the council tax for granted.'

Much is implied by the phrase 'the best way of using taxpayers' money to meet social goals'. This includes:

- clear goals – based on the mandate of the politicians, and other expressions of citizens' needs and demands (participatory democracy, direct citizens engagement, surveys, data on the use of existing services);
- deep transparency about how services are delivered, in the back office and the front office, in order to be able to identify how things can be done better;
- processes that realise to the full the capacity of staff to contribute to the quality of services;
- rigorous awareness of risk – not necessarily avoiding

it, but transparently and rationally weighing up costs and benefits so as to be prepared for foreseeable consequences, if after weighing the balance, the risk is taken.

There are many sources of wisdom on the techniques that can improve these procedures. The private sector is one of them, but so too are other experiences in the public sector and also the experiences or influences of other parts of the social sector, including trade unions, and social movements like the women's and environmental movements. A strength of the City Service team is that many of them have worked in the private sector and are clear-eyed about its weaknesses and sufficiently confident in the distinctive values and rationale of the public sector to be able to pick and mix techniques first used in the private sector for public sector goals.

In a local council such as Newcastle, we are dealing with a complex model that has its own logic relating to the maximisation of public benefit. This includes valuing any enhancement of the ability of public servants to achieve this maximisation. For example, one of the great advantages of the council delivering services itself, and hence retaining complete control, has been the way that City Service staff have gained immensely in experience – learning through doing (and through extra training) – enabling the council to use this knowledge for the future development of services and the council as a whole. The alternative would have meant that knowledge being privatised and re-presented as a profit-driven tender the next time round.

The public service business model based on the

maximisation of public benefit is no less clear and rigorous than any profit-based model. Indeed, the levels of scrutiny that are rightly involved if it is to be successful make it more demanding that the private sector model in many respects. Ray Ward sums it up: 'What the private company can say is that as long as we are adding shareholder value, share prices are looking good, profits are looking good, we're okay. We can't do that. The level of scrutiny is much higher, quite rightly because it is public funds.'

# Chapter 5

## It's the people, stupid: a new spirit of public sector management

'It's people's capability and commitment that needs to be released. These are assets not costs ... Managing people is a matter of ... true strategic importance. It's too important to be left solely to OD (organisational develop-ment).' So spoke City Service's new head Ray Ward. He was speaking at the 'City Service structure day', a gath-ering of all the City Service management to lay down the foundation of the 'City Service approach' for the management team in 2003.

He wasn't alone in his understanding of people as the key asset in the process of transforming services. 'It's the people, stupid' has been, in effect, a City Service motto. By 'people' is meant not only the council workers and deliverers of services, but also everyone who needs and uses these services. The way the leadership of City Service released the potential of this 'asset' – with the active support of a well-organised trade union, and the involvement of community groups – is the root of their ability to simultaneously achieve savings and bring about radical improvement.

So what was Newcastle City Council's approach to management? A meaningful answer to this must start in the work environment the City Service team inherited. It was an environment where procedures mattered more than purpose and people, non routine responses were greeted with a frown, staff immersed in isolating routines, and never encouraged to understand the wider context or importance of their work. A series of slides from Ray Ward's PowerPoint presentation at the City Service structure day told the story from the workers' perspective:

*'We have too much work to do ...'*
*'Our expertise is not recognised ...'*
*'Too much time is spent on admin and not on work ...'*
*'Our career expectations are not fulfilled ...'*
*'We are poorly informed ...'*
*'Senior management do not respond to or take our views seriously ...'*

This widespread dissatisfaction among the workforce had underpinned the trade unions' approach when they said not only 'no to privatisation' but 'the status quo is not an option'. Clearly, if this worker dissatisfaction was not addressed, any attempt at transformation would fail. In late 2002, the management reports to the council's cabinet, in which they formally recommended the creation of City Service, also pointed to the risks of a continuing lack of staff engagement and the possibility of non-acceptance of new working practices. .

## A break from elitism
In some contexts, managers would respond to this by tightening command structures and instilling fear as an instrument to achieve some kind of obedience. The

nature of relations between the trade union and City Service senior managers ruled out that option. Ray Ward and his colleagues summed up their approach like this: 'a thorough break with traditional management elitism'; 'sincere efforts to attract the commitment of the workforce'; 'a genuine reliance on worker initiative and creativity'.

This implied, Ray Ward's presentation continued, 'a reduction in managers' traditional conception of their right to manage – a shorthand for having the right to make decisions in ways that are unaccountable, undiscussable, and inconsistent', and 'a belief in the ethos of managers as servants.'

The aim, he said, was to become a learning organisation, learning from each other, from customers, from its environment.

## What did this mean in practice?

Take 'sincere efforts to attract the commitment of the workforce' – fundamental to this has been the commitment by management to a collaborative, problem-solving relationship with the union. It's been a grainy relationship, by no means smooth, as we shall see in the next chapter, but it has been essential to the momentum and accountability of the transformation process and to the self-confidence of the non-managerial staff within it. For Ray Ward and the senior leadership 'the union keeps us honest' – honest perhaps to the egalitarian ethos laid down as a foundation stone of City Service in the staff 'away day' held in their first formative months. This attitude to the union made regular and direct collaboration with the staff at every step of the change easier and more meaningful.

In every department, supported by Kath Moore's transformation team (see chapter 3), management conducted a detailed consultation with staff. This took place in a range of ways – pursuing 'workstreams' for every part of a service, following each task from initiation to completion; 'diagonal focus groups', which involved staff from every level in brainstorming ideas for improvement and change; regular staff forums; and regular, but less frequent, 'state of the nation' reports by Ray Ward, which communicated information back from the management to assemblies of all the staff.

## Coaches not commanders

And what did they mean by 'management is a servant?' Did such an idea have any relation to reality? City Service managers would say that it had to. As we've seen – and will see more as the change process got underway – a significant blockage to change lay in the old-style management hierarchies and cultures. Those driving change pursued a radically different approach to management and leadership.

Kath Moore, who had the job of devising and helping to implement strategies to break such blockages, sets the scene. 'We worked to develop new ways of leading, guided by what the staff were telling us,' she says. She recalls how, in response, 'some quite senior managers put up their hands and said that leading a fast-moving process of change wasn't for them. And they left, took voluntary redundancy.' A few, however, insisted that 'we have always managed these people this way and it's the right way and we have got no intention of changing'.

The problem here could not just be put down to individuals, with the implication that the solution was simply to replace them with others. Neither was it a matter of the old managers not understanding the new technology. The problem, Moore explains, was 'they had a completely different idea of leadership from the one that was needed. They worked with more of a command and control model, whereas what we were trying to develop was a kind of leadership that is about bringing people on, encouraging initiative. It's about recognising that leadership – that natural ability to influence and shape things – is going to exist at all levels across the organisation and that if you find such talent at a grade D level and the individual wants to get involved in managing the change, then your job is to encourage, whereas the response of the command and control type of manager would be to tell the individual to get back in their box.' To reinforce her point, Moore describes how, when the senior team members were discussing new job titles, they thought about calling team leaders 'coaches', 'because that's what we mean by leadership'.

Any designer or innovative worker involved in creating something or solving a problem will tell you that creativity involves divergent and convergent phases – a phase when you explore and experiment in any direction that seems promising, followed by the phase of focusing everything learnt on making a final plan to tackle the problem at hand. The City Service management experience is no exception.

For the divergent phase Ray Ward emphasised play and metaphors, to break down fear and make people – himself and other managers – feel at ease with the uncertainty they faced. This included the brainstorming across specialisms and traditional divisions of labour, and learning from all kinds of users of their services (other council departments, outside organisations and individual citizens) and from other staff. On the convergent side were what Kath Moore describes as 'cracking business skills', meaning the skills of decision-making and planning to put the new ideas into practice to give customers – citizens, businesses and other public organisations, best value for money. To nurture each aspect of creativity there was a stress on high levels of training, and on training as a continuing process.

## Risk aware, not risk averse

Another phrase for the underlying fear and paralysis that produces the familiar image – and reality – of inertia in local government is 'risk aversion or avoidance'. City Service emphasised a different approach – risk management – which does not necessarily avoid risk, but it still ensures awareness of it.

If risk avoidance is not uppermost, risks can sometimes be taken. If a risk might have a significant impact, then actions to reduce its likelihood and/or impact can be considered. 'The point is to know the risks in a project, prioritise them and then put things in place to make sure that the risk isn't realised and it doesn't become an issue,' explains Lisa Clark, the member of the team responsible for risk management in City Service decision-making.

'You can take positive risks too,' she adds cheerfully, having just taken one in transferring 7,000 staff onto a new email system with only an hour's briefing, a handout and online training, rather than the normal classroom approach – which would have been impossible for 7,000 people. In this case she had mitigated the risk of disaster on day one of the new system by working with different council departments to identify 'superusers' – personal assistants, for example, whose job depended on email – and offering them a two-day classroom training course so that they could act as champions and support others in their areas. They also had drop-in sessions, telephone advice and special training, and all went well on the day. 'It was quite innovative for us as the council,' she says. The email system change wasn't strictly part of the City Service transformation but Lisa's management of it was typical of a City Service approach.

City Service was effectively mandated to overcome the risk-averse culture that was widespread throughout the council. Lisa Clark again: 'Because we were going through such a high level of change and transformation, it was almost as if we were given permission to take risk.' The whole project of City Service was a 'a bold decision', in treasurer Paul Woods' words, so its practice could be equally bold.

Creating a risk management culture that could permeate the entire service while it was changing, and afterwards, involved identifying risks that might prevent the team from achieving its objectives, and speaking the truth without fear and on the basis of mutual respect to all those affected. Risk management also emphasised the continual review of risk factors, rather than one-off judgements, along with the idea that everyone in a project should concern themselves with the risks attached to it. Risk management was demystified, so that it wasn't seen as some technical trick or bureaucratic procedure, but as a means of being more in control of, and less at the mercy of, events. Finally a corporate risk management group made up of City Service managers took overall responsibility for constantly reviewing risks and ensuring that the methodology became second nature.

Some projects presented risks of mega proportions. Take the timing of the switching on of the SX3 system for processing benefits and council tax debt recovery. The stakes were enormous, affecting some of the most vulnerable people in society. The normal systems would be offline for six weeks while data was migrated to the new system. Some 33,000 benefit claims would have to be paid manually, and six weeks of cheques had to be got ready, while £170 million pounds of council tax recovery was also at stake.

Whoever gave the final go ahead on this was giving potentially career-breaking advice. Moreover, they had to convince auditors who were looking for certainty and accustomed to a culture of risk aversion. Not surprisingly the risk management was carried out with a meticulous attention to detail. Switchover proceeded but it was not risk-free. The fact that it had to be taken at the same time as a decision about going live with a new payroll system, affecting the salary payments of 15,000 people, only added to the potential difficulties. These risks had to be assessed and taken at the same time as maintaining the everyday business of the department.

One of the auditors who needed to be convinced was Joe Blue, located in the office across the corridor from the treasurer, Paul Woods. Joe is every inch the popular image of an auditor, with his sharp eyes, his evident enthusiasm for a craft that others might find dull, his precise memory of the experience and his pride that procedure had been followed all the way to the final green light. He identified with the decision; like his colleague Paul Woods he seems to have been convinced by the City Service approach.

Risk management is not risk erasure, however. There have been occasions when City Service has taken a risk that has led part of a project to fail and the project manager has had to think again – such as in the case of the outsourcing of document scanning in revenues and benefits. Every night a van would take documents to Rotherham to be scanned and electronically returned. But this process was too slow and inflexible. Staff needed to be able to scan the documents more speedily and closer to their dealings with customers. The traffic light system that alerted the Programme Board – the group of senior managers leading the change – to problems went red, the task was taken in-house and lessons were learnt.

## Purpose driven pragmatism

Since the days when a high-risk project in a risk-averse culture meant muttered predictions of doom, City Service has won considerable respect. One source of this respect has been that although the City Service management are no respecters of procedure for its own sake, they haven't so much cut corners as redesigned them openly and accountably. Although they can come to seem to be set in stone, all procedures are humanly designed and can therefore be humanly redesigned. One example is home working. Staff wanted the possibility of choosing that option – it would save on accommodation too – but internal procedures did not allow for it. After discussions with staff and union reps, Peter Bowers, the head of organisational development, rewrote the procedures.

The same purpose-driven pragmatism has been been at the root of City Service's approach to the adoption of tried and tested techniques for managing projects and overall programmes. These include, in particular, the 'PRINCE 2' and MSP (Managing Successful Programmes) management strategies. PRINCE 2 is the name of the set of techniques recognised throughout local government as best practice guidance for planning, organising, managing and completing a project.

'It is mostly about clear and strategic thinking,' remarks transformation programme manager Julia

Woollard, herself an impressively clear and firm thinker. But handing over a vast primer on PRINCE 2, Woollard also remarks that a person could 'master every detail from page one to page 500 and do every single piece of paperwork that PRINCE 2 recommends – fill in their quality log, their risk log, their exception reports, their traffic-light reports ... and the project could still fail if they're not good at working with people and managing a team.'

On the other hand, she continues, 'you can have someone who doesn't use PRINCE 2 at all but is a great project manager because they really know what they want to do, they logically think through what needs to happen and in what order, they're good at getting people on side, and they just make things happen'. She concludes: 'We've tried to find a middle ground where project managers get on with leading their teams and delivering the project and we support them in ensuring that the project is underpinned with a solid foundation of best practice tools, techniques and documentation.' An important part of this support has been training on a continuing basis, for which City Service has won an award from UK Skills.

## Life and leadership beyond hierarchy

This commitment to a supportive form of management, a move away from command and control, has been one side of a dual aspect to effective and radical changes in the City Service transformation. The other side has been the elimination of layers of supervision, and the reversal of the existing deferment of decisions upwards, a behaviour associated with centralised command structures. Change brought a much needed transfer of responsibility away from the centre to the point at which a particular issue or problem arises. The structures that City Service agreed at its special 'awayday' were relatively 'flat' – they favour carrying expertise across boundaries to solve problems. The focus is on the service being self-organising, with an emphasis on learning and guided by the ethos that 'it is better to ask for forgiveness than to ask for permission'. The whole set up is based on a desire to communicate and collaborate laterally with less emphasis on hierarchy.

This approach had benefits throughout the programme. Many leaders emerged from beneath the hierarchies – 'hidden in the directorates', as one City Service manager put it. These were people who thrived in the problem-solving teams that brought people together with little regard for hierarchy to solve a problem or run a project. Several of them went on to lead projects or sections themselves. In a sense they are the first generation of managers in Newcastle directly trained by the distinctive City Service approach and passing it on by practical example.

The pushing of initiative and responsibility away from the centre has been such a strong and systematic feature of City Service that it has begun to transform the centre of the department (i.e. City Service) from a traditional model of management in local government into a hub from which management support numerous, largely autonomous projects and activities. A new kind of public sector organisation has emerged, with a leadership role that is more about facilitation and developing a shared direction than it is about exercising control. The implications of this for local government organisation more generally are immense. And already the rest of Newcastle City Council is beginning to take them on board.

This model of many autonomous but interconnected projects and initiatives taking place simultaneously as part of a common programme was one of the keys to the success of the City Service transformation process. It was a complex operation, which included overseeing 23 projects with overlapping timetables; running the day-to-day work of five different businesses (sections of City Service), and bringing about organisational change in all of them; delivering new IT systems; and allocating resources between competing priorities. Moreover, many of the services themselves were becoming more complex in what they provided as they became easier for citizens to access

This is the other side of a phenomenon increasingly recognised in organisational theory and practice – that centralisation tends to simplify. In some contexts this makes centralisation an appropriate move – for example, in the case of City Service, the centralisation of human resources and payroll functions from all the directorates into one section. But in other contexts it can lower the quality of the service or the efficiency of the process (for example, with the transformation process itself, or with the organisation of the customer service centres, in which expert frontline staff now have considerable autonomy, as we will see later). In these increasingly prevalent contexts, the more that initiative and responsibility is distributed, the more likely the system is to be efficient, given a supportive framework and environment.

In Newcastle, an essential aspect of a supportive environment was provided by the fact that the union had signed up for the change, but this was conditional on a new kind of management. *The two reinforced each other.* The union pushed strongly for the in-house bid on the basis not only that it was an alternative to privatisation but that it would involve change in management culture and personnel. Tony Carr a full time union rep during the transformation was clear that the methods of management that led to the need for change could not successfully lead the council forward.

## Porous to democratic pressures

City Service began its life as the result of a high profile, long-worked-for political decision. From the start, considerations of democracy have been part of its culture in several ways.

First, there is accountability to the elected council. This involves more than the formal reports of City Service head Ray Ward to the council executive. Two councillors were active members of a new steering committee established specifically to enable and drive the transformation programme. One of them, Anita Lower, the council cabinet member responsible for transformation and modernisation, says: 'I often met up with City Service staff and managers to discuss particular issues. The whole set up was very open and transparent. It made it it easy for me to see how the work was being done.' A closer relationship than is often the case between elected members and staff; and one made easier by the consciously open way that City Service is managed.

Another aspect of City Service's relationship with elected members has been through the council's 'scrutiny committee', which was established to make council officials account for the way they implement council decisions. Ray Ward frequently faced questions from the scrutiny committee.

He remembers vividly what happened when the new system for managing the thousands of documents that passed through revenues and benefits failed to perform as expected and consequently benefits were not being processed on time and problems arose with council tax collection: 'I was being called to scrutiny meetings, to the Your Homes Newcastle board [Newcastle Council's 'arms length management company', which managed what was the city's public housing], to the tenants federation meetings, executive meetings and all the committee meetings to explain over and over again why the benefits performance was stubbornly not performing, why they should believe me and what we were going to do. For six to nine months my life was just managing that interface, message and accountability.'

'I am not being critical,' he adds. 'This is what it is all about, you are dealing with some of the most vulnerable

people in society and you need to do it right. The councillors focused on the outcomes and wanted to know
why the performance wasn't good enough. A negative
result can affect your electability.'

City Service's ethos and way of working has encouraged a more respectful relationship with service users,
breaking from the tradition of treating them as passive
recipients of what public servants believe is good for
them. Its more egalitarian organisation has meant that
almost all staff are aware of how their work contributes
to meeting the public's needs and are more motivated to
give a responsive service.

The City Service story has laid bare the workings of
management of public services, revealing things to be
pliable that often seem inexorably rigid. There has been
much public policy debate about, and experiments with,
citizen participation as a means of strengthening democratic control,[1] and there is now a belated interest in user
and staff collaboration (sometimes known as 'co-production') to improve the day-to-day quality of services in
which users can be actively involved (schools, doctors'
surgeries, recycling and so on). But the systems and
culture of the management of the council's employees
and resources has rarely been discussed in terms of
whether it facilitates or hinders democratic control.

The City Service story, and the unusual combination
of people who made it possible, points to the importance
of the *way a public service is managed* for the ability of
elected members and voters to have an influence. It
demonstrates that a circuitry of relationships can be

created so that a live current can flow from the mandate of the elected politician to the frontline staff responding to the needs of the citizen, via the support of the back office staff and management. Vital to this is transparency and a building of relations of collaboration and mutual respect rather than hierarchies of command and control. Fundamental to such an open and egalitarian approach has been the role of the trade union.

1. Newcastle Council for example has been piloting a process of youth participation in budget allocations for youth activities and facilities for 3 years and in 2008 spreading the experiment from three to five wards.

# Chapter 6

## The union: making management accountable

One of City Service's greatest assets from the outset was the wholehearted commitment of the union – leaders and members – to the transformation. The campaign for the in-house bid had effectively percolated a desire for change throughout the Newcastle City Council workforce, diffusing it to every section and employee. As UNISON branch secretary Kenny Bell put it: 'The staff had won a victory; they were up for change.'

As their side of the deal, management agreed to work with the union to involve the staff at every stage and every level, and to avoid compulsory redundancies by managing job losses through redeployment, retraining and voluntary redundancy. The extent of staff and union involvement in the changes, and the resources – including time – given to retraining, redeployment and voluntary redundancy packages, were unprecedented, certainly for Newcastle, and probably compared with other local authorities.

The unions were intensely involved from having an important say in the appointment of new senior managers through every step of the change. 'The union' meant the 30 or so union reps for the different sections of what had been ITRS and was now City Service, plus UNISON branch secretary Kenny Bell and Tony Carr as union convenor for City Service.

## A central role

In the first two years Tony Carr played a central role. We met him in chapter 3, an enthusiastic easy-going man in his late thirties keen to make things work and work fairly – and always willing to explain what was going on to whoever asked. One feature of the transformation process was the need to invent new institutions, fit for the purpose of driving change, and find people who could make the most of the new roles that this created.

This is exactly what happened to consolidate the role of the union so that it enabled staff fully to play a positive role in the transformation process and ensure that their interests were well represented. The UNISON branch committee negotiated for a full-time secondment to a trade union post dedicated to representing staff in the transformation process. They nominated Tony Carr for the job.

A full-time secondment was unusual for a department of only 650 staff. The normal job of a trade union rep, dealing with daily grievances, minor disputes, pensions and the like wouldn't warrant full-time secondment for such a small number, but the trade union role in the transformation needed someone to take an overview, and to work with all the reps and shadow the managers at every stage. Tony Carr estimates he spent 20 per cent of his time in this new post dealing with everyday grievances in City Service and 80 per cent on the transformation.

Throughout the changes trade union representation was organised to mirror the structure of City Service.

Each division head would meet with the trade union representatives in their division on a fortnightly basis. 'So,' explains Tony Carr, 'Lisa Marshall and other trade union reps in revenues and benefits would meet the head of revenues and benefits, and the exchequer service reps would meet with Steve Evans and so on. It was a pretty open relationship; it wasn't a case of being dictated to.'

This intercommunication during the transformation programme meant a close day-to-day relationship between Tony and the leader of the transformation team, Kath Moore. Tony describes how in his role as full-time union convenor he effectively shadowed Kath: 'At all of the meetings Kath was at, I was there. I sat alongside her. Sometimes you wondered which side you were working on. It was strange, it was a new way of working. The commitment involved wasn't just a paper commitment, we were really involved.'

## The role of the union

In the context of such a relationship between management and staff – so open that the union convenor felt 'strange' and not sure what side he was on – what exactly was the role of the union? There was a commitment to working jointly, but where did the union actually exercise influence, and how?

For a start, the union influenced the kind of people who were employed in the key management roles – the importance of the union's commitment and involvement in the process was made clear to new managers when they were appointed. Three out of six senior managers, Ray Ward, Kath Moore and Steve Evans, were recruited into City Service. (The other three had been managers under the old ITRS arrangement.)

All short-listed candidates had to go through what became known as 'trial by vol-au-vent'. 'There was a buffet lunch and then there were staff groups, who had obviously been briefed to come round and talk to each of the candidates and sound us out,' remembers Steve Evans, also recalling his nerves that day. 'I'd not come across that before and I didn't manage to eat much of my lunch.'

What the union reps were looking out for as they talked to the candidates nervously nibbling at their vol-au-vents, was whether they recognised the importance of the unions, whether they were open to dialogue with the unions and what was their experience and knowledge of change management. 'This was important for the candidates,' says Kenny Bell. 'It meant they knew the importance of the unions in the process.' The union subsequently put its views to the interviewing panel. Union and management were in agreement on the final choices

The union made it clear that it would not manage the change. That was management's job: to draw up the proposals, to be responsible for implementing them on time and to meet the agreed goals. Even so, the union's role went beyond the normal situation in local government, where unions are usually only consulted when management's plans have implications for job content and structure.

Another distinctive contribution of the union to the transformation was its organising ability: a skilled, trained capacity to facilitate staff engagement. 'We help bring people together round an issue, with a sense that it's part of something bigger. We build confidence that they can do something and strengthen the understanding of a common purpose,' explains Josie Bird, UNISON branch chair. 'The first hurdle is to convince members that they do have a voice, that it's worth having an opinion because it will have an impact. That way people will get a sense of shared control and make the issue theirs.'

## Building trust and testing moments

From the outset, every step of change was discussed with union reps before being opened up to wider consultation. Then the reps would be available to support members with problems or complaints about the changes in finding a mutually agreeable solution with management. There was a more or less explicit agreement that neither side would spring surprises on the other. There was also agreement that they both work to ensure staff received a consistent message about what was going on. So Kath Moore and Joanne Moss, the communications officer on the business and transformation team, met to discuss the content of the regular City Service newsletter with Carr, to ensure that there were no mixed messages coming from management's and the union's communications.

It was vital for the effective working of this process that management did not see staff disagreement as nega-

tive. And there was plenty of it. Kenny Bell remembers:
'Time and time again we would go through a process of
thorough discussion with management [and] the union
reps and their members. There would sometimes be
whole days in work groups and one to one discussions,
which led to new solutions, ways round problems or the
reaching of a consensus.'

This ease and trust had to be built, and in the early
days there were some testing moments. A key one that
firmed up management's recognition of the importance
of discussing plans with the union leadership and
section reps before making decisions occurred in City
Service's first year, before many of the key relationships
and communication processes were in place. It was over
the cashiers – the 20 or so women responsible for taking
residents' payments of rents and council tax.

These women had been based in the neighbourhood
housing offices. Though scattered across the city, they
had strong bonds through a pride in their work. Ann
Brown, who became their union rep, sums it up: 'I was
always very proud of the work that I did. We didn't open
till 8.30am and there would be people in the queue by
7.50 because the neighbourhood office was very much a
community meeting place.' With the new plans for
customer service centres and the increased variety of
ways people could pay their rents and council tax – via
post offices and shops, online and so on – the cashiers'
original jobs were to go. The transition to new jobs at the
customer service centres and at the Civic was going to
be a sensitive one, requiring discussion, representation

and preparation. Instead, they heard the news, in Ann Brown's words, 'like a bombshell'.

She describes the reaction: 'We were really, really angry. We felt we were all doing such a good job and we didn't see why they would make us feel so threatened. We just wanted explanations, to know what was going on.' City Service head Ray Ward faced a hostile meeting and an angry Kenny Bell, who Ann Brown had asked to come and represent the cashiers and who felt the union should have been involved from the beginning.

In the end the women were satisfied with the final outcome. It's not the same at the Civic or in one of the customer service centres, where they now work, but Ann Brown reflects: 'There are things about it that I still enjoy. I still work with the same girls and the customers. I have been quite lucky in a way. We have really achieved what we wanted to do. People are using direct debits and other methods of payment, a bit like my children doing everything online – you can't live in the past.' For the City Service leadership, the experience with the cashiers was something of a turning point in understanding the importance of working on equal terms with the union.

The union, in turn, knew that the threat of outsourcing was always there if the transformation programme faltered. On several occasions reps had to remind members that they had signed up for the deal and could not go back on it, so long as management honoured its side of it.

How did they put the argument? 'We stressed the importance of recognising that long term security lay with improving services,' says Kenny Bell. 'In meetings the majority knew that one way or another they were secure even if their jobs were changing, so improvement drives people. The importance of change was understood. Most UNISON members were residents as well, paying council tax and depending on council services. For the success of this, it was very important that staff could see that managers' minds were open, they were willing to be challenged.'

## The power of the union

In fact, the power of the union was a constant presence in the background, acting as a guarantor of the employment conditions that led staff to feel able to be creatively involved in a process of change that was to transform their working lives. As Ray Ward puts it, 'I was under no illusion that if we got things wrong and if we didn't respond, Kenny would escalate the issue. I've no doubt about that. But we have reached a point where Kenny will say "Let's work to fix this, let's do what we've always done." We've built something that is worth perpetuating. I value it, I know they value it and have a willingness and the ability to do it.'

The agreement the union had negotiated on retraining, redeployment and the avoidance of compulsory redundancies further underpinned the union's role as guarantor; it meant that staff weren't paralysed by fear and insecurity through the transformation process. Management agreed to give at least one year's notice to enable people to find alternative employment in the council, and the human resources department gave every support necessary, including retraining, to avoid compulsory redundancies.

According to Kenny Bell: 'The benefits of people being more involved in their work is widely understood in terms of higher quality performance and so on, but what is not recognised, and in many contexts doesn't exist, is the [role as] guarantor and security that a trade union can provide behind all this. That's what we've delivered in City Service. It makes all the positives you can get from engaging the workforce – improvements, changes and so on – more sustainable ... Members came to us if there was a problem, if they weren't happy with the type of consultation that was going on or with the consequences of the new systems'. When that happened the union and management worked together to find solutions.

Kenny concludes: 'We have acted as an overseer, a monitor of that environment ... It's our job to keep the management accountable, not so much to the staff, but to the change.'

# Chapter 7

## Employing the private sector on the terms of the public

### Does the private sector have a role in this new environment?

The in-house bid at Newcastle included provision for contracting a partner to 'procure hardware and software, expertise and capacity in areas of change management' and to do so through a process of 'knowledge transfer to sustain our self-sufficiency'. From the beginning, the emphasis in this relationship was on council control. For all the talk of 'partnership', the reality was an employer-contractor relationship. And it was a tough one. To prove it Julia Woollard, who was responsible for day-to-day management of the contract on behalf of City Service, has a thick file of invoices she challenged from the main contractor Fujitsu. Negotiation and careful contract management throughout the transformation programme has saved City Service a significant amount of money.

The first calling in of skills from the private sector was to draw up a timed plan of implementation. City Service hired the PA Consulting Group to work quickly with chief executive Ray Ward and head of the business, development and transformation team Kath Moore to develop the necessary timetable and plan for how resources would be mobilised. PA was hired specifically for this job, although probably the company would have liked to play a key role in the implementation of the programme as well. But, as, Julia Woollard explains 'I think that it worked out well that we used one organisation to develop what the programme would look like and then went out to tender for delivery. It meant that the programme was "pure" rather than developed by the company that would also play an important role in delivering it.'

During the implementation of the transformation programme, the key gap for the council lay in the skills and bargaining power needed to procure new IT systems on the best terms. This proved to be where a private contractor was most useful. The City Service team also decided it needed to get advice and expertise on the best techniques for managing a programme with such a high risk of failure and such high stakes, but here there was a strong emphasis on transferring the expertise to the council. In the tendering process Fujitsu's bid was the only one that came in below the City Service affordability sum of £7.72 million.

## A flexible and favourable contract

City Service negotiated a very favourable 'guaranteed maximum price' (GMP) contract to ensure that there was no unforeseen overspend. This is a contract in which the employer (in this case City Service, on behalf of the council) spells out the work it wants from the contractor (Fujitsu) for a maximum price. City Service then paid invoices on the basis of agreed milestones throughout the delivery of each individual project within the overall contract. No payment was made without specific authorisation.

The great advantage for City Service was that under a GMP contract the contractor cannot charge for extra costs incurred in delivering an agreed project. If a system cost more than Fujitsu had advised in the tender, then Fujitsu would pay the extra cost. However, it was not a guaranteed minimum price contract – so if a system cost less than advised in the tender, the council only paid the actual cost.

In this sense all risk was with Fujitsu, and it drove effective partnership working between Fujitsu and the council as it was in everyone's interest to deliver projects quickly to the agreed high standards. To reinforce this responsibility for the risks, Fujitsu provided written assurances that it would underwrite delivery failure by fellow partners or any sub-contractors (its role was partly to manage other suppliers, especially of hardware). This commitment proved to be very important early in the programme when the document management system procured by Fujitsu for managing the shift from paper to electronic documents, and the continuing electronic organisation of these documents, failed to live up to expectations, causing severe problems, especially for those working in revenues and benefits. Fujitsu replaced the system at its own, considerable, cost.

Another favourable feature of the contract with Fujitsu was that it allowed City Service scope for manoeuvre and flexibility on the detail of the individual projects. For example, as we'll see in the next chapter, City Service decided to employ Jeff Pasternack directly as a project manager, rather than have a manager from Fujitsu, as had been planned originally. The cost of direct employment was lower, so money was saved that could be spent elsewhere.

A key feature of how City Service handled the transformation programme at Newcastle was the way it combined having a clear goal and direction with a willingness and ability to work with – even relish – uncertainty. Both flexibility and a clear framework were essential in such a major contract, and as Kath Moore, Julia Woollard and the rest of transformation team with whom Fujitsu worked gained in confidence and clarity about exactly where the expertise of the private sector was essential, they were able to continually to adapt the relationship with the company to the changing needs of City Service.

## The view from Fujitsu

How did Fujitsu feel about this contract? Based in their offices in Silverlink, a somewhat sterile industrial estate between Newcastle and North Tyneside, Ian Lumley is the current manager of Fujitsu's account with City Service. There have been a number of Fujitsu managers working with Newcastle over the lifetime of the transformation programme and although relations have not always been easy, since Ian and his colleague Erica Lawrie took over in 2006 there has been a close working relationship with the City Service team.

Ian Lumley admits that 'the Newcastle contract is slightly unusual', explaining that most of Fujitsu's contracts 'are on a risk and reward basis. With the Newcastle project, we take all the risk.' Was it worth it? 'We take a long term view,' he answers. 'If it is ten years before we gain any benefits, so be it. We do a tough business appraisal of everything we take on. We need a clear end point and to know that the project is achievable and profitable.'

He said the guaranteed maximum price contract was viable 'because City Service had a very clear idea of what they wanted'. Asked whether Fujitsu would do it again, in spite of the costs it had to cover, his reply was positive, because of the long-term benefits, which included the possibility of future work for Newcastle City Council. The company had an earlier contract with the council, servicing the old mainframe computer. It was a relationship it wanted to keep and a basis for other contracts with councils in the northeast. The council was in a strong bargaining position.

It was not only the contract and the way City Service managed it that made the most of this strength. In the transfer of knowledge, too, City Service made sure it adapted what Fujitsu had to offer for its own purposes. In addition to the procurement of technology systems, Fujitsu also had expertise in techniques of programme and project management, with all its associated components: anticipating and planning for risks, understanding interdependencies, integrating the stakeholders and so on. Here Fujitsu passed on some useful technical know-how. But Julia Woollard and her colleagues took a robustly pragmatic view of the associated management techniques, recognising that they were mostly about clear and strategic thinking, rather than anything magical.

As well as Fujitsu, City Service had a couple of other encounters with private consultants – in one case a company employed for a specific and limited auditing task, and in another case one whose services were turned down. About this insiders remarked, off the record, 'They really didn't tell us anything we didn't know'.

Transformation programme manager Julia Woollard sums up the generally discriminating view of private contractors that City Service built up from experience: 'There's a view that you pay consultants a lot of money because they know much more than you. But when you're exposed to them, you realise that it's very specific expertise that's the most valuable. In general, you are best placed to understand your organisation, identify the barriers to change and bring stakeholders on board. If you have limited resources, it's most effective to target them on buying in specific services and capacity where the private sector has an advantage and can really add value.'

Where, in the experience of City Service, has this proved to be the case? The answer is generally in the area of procurement. 'Using Fujitsu to undertake procurements definitely streamlined the process and we benefited from their expertise and buying power,' comments Julia Woollard. This did not, however, mean handing the procurement process over to Fujitsu. City Service staff developed a rigorous methodology for evaluating different systems, giving weighted consideration to how efficiently they functioned, how they would be implemented and supported, their 'look and feel' and various technical factors. The process of applying these criteria, including visits to sites where the relevant systems were being used, involved staff who would be using the technology. Fujitsu would then produce a procurement document recommending a purchase, which went to a 'challenge meeting' to ensure the right decision.

Fujitsu's Ian Lumley remarks on a tendency among public sector managers when they outsource 'to throw the problem over the wall'. In Newcastle, however, even in the area where Fujitsu's expertise was most valued – hardware and software procurement – Fujitsu found itself working very much on the same side of the wall, in harness with – and accountable to – public sector managers.

# Chapter 8

## Ch ch ch changes ...

### PART ONE: SNAKES AND LADDERS

You never quite know with City Service what's serious and what's fun. The ambivalence is intentional, a way of disturbing the icing sugar on the desk (see City Service head Ray Ward's 'icing sugar test', chapter 3). 'Often we are not aware of the need to change things,' explains Ray. 'We know what we do, but until what is going wrong is summed up and presented to us, we think we're doing all right.' One of Ray Ward's tactics in the projects he has been involved in has been to have some fun – for instance, drawing a picture of a roller coaster to show the benefits system that he was galvanising staff in Hereford to sort out. It was going up and down and looping the loop, with people falling out and being sick. 'I was just trying to say "Well, that's how our benefits claimants feel,"' he explains.

At one of his first meetings with the rest of the City Service team he introduced the idea of a game of snakes and ladders as a metaphor for what needed to be done. 'You see how many ladders there are, you see how many snakes there are,' he told his colleagues. 'What we've got to do is to focus on the snakes.' At first some people found it a bit patronising, he says. 'But they get into game playing mode – people are quite competitive, and if you use a game as a metaphor, they start to join in. If you say, "How are we going to get rid of these snakes?" they suddenly want to do it, whereas if you say, "We've got several closed-process items here, how do we remove them?" it's just not fun, is it?'

## The unresponsiveness of existing services

Snake number one facing City Service was the way the council related to the people it was meant to serve. We've seen how unresponsive people often found it: requiring a trek round the corridors of the Civic if they had more than one issue with council services at a time, long waits before phones were answered. Audrey Shakespeare, a local resident from the west end of the city, summed it up in chapter 1: 'You often didn't get the correct information, they wouldn't put you onto the right department you wanted to get through to. If you went into the local housing office, you didn't get much information out of them. Even if you phoned up you still didn't get quite the information you were looking for.'

To drive out this particular snake it was determined that the transformed services should aim to make sure that enquiries were resolved by the first person the enquirer came into contact with. City Service would consider its processes 'from the viewpoint of its customers'. This amounted to 'an organisational culture new to the council', according to Ray Ward.

The viewpoint of customers was not homogenous, however. Extensive consultation – including surveys and visits by City Service staff to ward committees and local residents groups – showed that around two thirds of the city's residents preferred to contact the council and pay bills by phone while one third still treasured personal face-to-face interaction. But on one issue there was near unanimity: the desire for a 'one stop shop' for access to all council services. 'Everyone said they would like them [services] to be in district shopping centres where there was already, say, a GP or a library, so they could deal with everything under one roof,' the consultation reported.

Responding to these two streams of opinion, City Service created a new contact centre (for contact by phone, fax or email) and new customer service centres where people could walk in and access a wide range of services.

## The contact centre

The contact centre was established in March 2006 to enable residents to get in touch with the council, from 8am to 6pm, by phone, email or fax. The way it works is indicative of the way City Service has adapted private sector techniques selectively for public sector ends.

A call centre is an archetypal private sector invention. Indeed, the manager of Newcastle's contact centre, Alison Johnson, was recruited from the Newcastle call centre of the financial firm Zurich. She left the private sector because of her frustration with efficiency drives that included limiting the length of calls with customers. Her ambition in joining Newcastle City Council was to create something unencumbered by either the worst traits of public sector restrictiveness or profit-driven service reduction. She wanted to work from scratch to establish a contact centre based on 'best principles'.

The service targets of the contact centre were agreed following an extensive consultation with 700 people in all of the city's wards. The aim is to answer all calls within 60 seconds. Callers are presented with just two options before they can speak to someone directly – not an endless phone tree where they are asked to press 1, 2, 3 or 4' and then again 'press 1, 2, 3' and so on. Calls are timed but the policy of the contact centre is not, unlike many private sector centres, to end them within a set time. The policy is to resolve callers' problems, no matter how long it takes.

## The customer service centres

Meanwhile, Newcastle's pre-existing network of 21 neighbourhood housing offices was to be replaced by a much smaller number of newly built 'customer service centres' where local people could speak to council staff in person. Although the neighbourhood housing offices were popular with some people (as we heard from Ann Brown in chapter 6), who could use them to pay council tax or rent personally, they were very expensive in relation to the few transactions that some of them handled per day. Additionally, 'some were in a deplorable state and quite inaccessible for anyone with a disability. They weren't DDA [Disability Discrimination Act] compliant,' remembers Helen Batey, who had worked in a housing office for many years before becoming head of customer services.

Six new customer care centres were planned eventually to replace most of the neighbourhood housing offices. By the winter of 2008, all six had opened. This meant that the number of points for face-to-face contact was reduced (though a number of the busier neighbourhood housing offices have remained open) but the variety of services accessible from customer service centres is far greater than neighbourhood housing offices were able to deliver. And residents can now use the customer service centres, or more than 150 payment outlets in post offices or newsagents, to pay their council tax or utility bills.

Up to 90 different council services can be accessed at the customer service centres, along with those of other public service agencies, such as the NHS. The Kenton customer service centre is typical in that it contains a GP practice, a library, a physiotherapy unit, a social services office and representatives from Your Homes Newcastle, the arms-length management organisation (ALMO) with responsibility for 31,000 council homes in the city. The co-location of existing services in customer service centres has in some instances led to a large increase in the number of people using them compared to the numbers of people who used the local housing offices. When the neighbourhood library was moved into the Outer West customer service centre in Denton, for example, a 115 per cent increase in visitors resulted.

## Public customers

Embedded in the culture of City Service is a commitment to customer service that has drawn on established private sector practice. 'We are working in a customer care environment,' one City Service employee commented. 'It's almost like going into a shop – the customer is always right. We've got to be seen to be professional; we've got to be seen to be providing a service. In some ways, maybe we have become like the private sector, and realised that the people out there are paying our wages and expect a service of a certain quality.'

But while City Service took what it needed from the private sector, it did not indiscriminately mimic private sector practice. What was adopted was also adapted to meet the needs of a public service ethos.

## Customer relationship management

This discerning way of dealing with ideas and practices imported from the private sector can be seen in the adaptation of customer relationship management (CRM) software, to the council's needs.

CRM is utilised for different purposes in the public sector. 'The big difference between both sectors can often lie in the way in which each regards the customer,' explains Eric Bohl, the director of customer service at Tower Hamlets Council in London. 'In the private sector the level of service given to each customer is sometimes seen to be based upon his or her current or perceived future value to the organisation. This can mean that CRM is used to ensure high-value customers get a higher level of service than low-value customers ... In the public sector each customer is valued equally. The sector's goal is to provide each customer with a service tailored to his or her needs. CRM can ensure that dealing with a council is simple, that the customer's needs are understood and that councils deliver the correct services to address them.'

As Steven Scott, a customer service centre supervisor in Newcastle, points out, 'People have a choice in the private sector. We don't have a choice when it comes to local authority services; these are services people need – we don't want to exclude members of the community at all. We are very conscious that it is important we make all our services accessible to all.'

Introduced in November 2002 at a cost of less than £1 million, Newcastle's CRM system was aimed at changing people's experience of the council. When people first make contact, their personal details are recorded. Subsequent enquiries at customer service centres are also registered so that their case histories are available to customer service staff and they do not have to repeat their original requests or queries. Staff can also see what other services customers might need and make sure all the relevant information and availability is offered.

CRM enables generic frontline staff at customer service centres either to resolve problems themselves, or to arrange for the customer to speak by phone to a specialist, without the customer having to visit staff working in different parts of the council – often in separate buildings. When it is necessary, frontline staff can arrange an appointment with specialist staff, if possible there and then, if the inquiry is made at the Civic.

By working with the suppliers, Lagan, moreover, the CRM system adopted by the council was modified to allow access to the computer systems of different council departments, such as those dealing with council tax and housing benefit. Through a technique known as 'screen scraping', multiple screens in the back office system were reformatted into a smaller number of screens to permit frontline staff to deal with enquiries.

'Scripting' – a series of instructions to guide staff through the completion of the inquiry – was also developed and built into the use of the CRM to ensure that staff untrained in particular specialist areas could navigate through individual cases. The two script writers, Bill Morton and Jean Kent, ensconced in a friendly little office in the customer service centre by the side of the Civic, worked with every conceivable scenario – developing their scripts in response to real-life scenarios encountered by receptionists and adapting them as a result of feedback from frontline staff and consultation with the public. The resulting guide (which is not in fact an exact script) supports staff in responding to public inquires. Extra expertise was also drawn into frontline services by importing some staff into customer services from back office departments, such as planning.

'When we started, the rest of the staff thought they would never be able to deliver the level of service that customers expect without having specialist staff on the front line,' says Christine Herriot, head of efficiency at Newcastle. 'But through the use of technology, and by sharing the tacit knowledge of individuals, we give them the confidence to be able to deliver the services.'

The main effect of CRM was to speed up the resolution of enquiries. Before its introduction, frontline staff had to be trained how to operate 40 different IT systems used by various council departments. Access was slow because each system was separately organised and password-controlled. In 2002, 40 per cent of enquiries at the Civic's customer service centre (at the time the only one open) were dealt with at first point of contact. By December 2007, data from four customer services centres showed that 89.8 per cent of enquiries were resolved by the first person an enquirer spoke to. Staff in back office departments were freed from dealing with routine enquiries but still 'on call' should they be required for one-to-one contact with customers.

'The introduction of CRM revolutionised what we could do in the customer service centres,' says Christine Herriot. 'The staff felt empowered and the customers satisfied.'

## Efficiency is meeting needs not ticking boxes

Although one of the benefits of CRM was efficiency, the driving ethos of City Service was never about processing large volumes of customers as quickly as possible. 'A lot of people come in with enquiries and they are completely unaware that what they are asking has nothing to do with the council,' says customer service centre manager Julie Cable. 'You don't just say "No". If somebody comes in looking for voluntary work, if you

## CRM opens up Newcastle Council

The introduction of the customer relationship management (CRM) IT system has meant that 90 council services are now available at customer service centres, ranging from council tax and housing benefits to electoral registration, schools' admissions and disabled parking badges. A new resident of Newcastle could, in one visit to a customer service centre:

- Apply for housing benefit
- Join the electoral register
- Find out what their water bill is
- Check their council tax and apply for council tax benefit
- Find out their waste collection day
- Arrange a bulky rubbish collection
- Apply for a skip licence
- Get a list of schools for their children, and find out if their children qualify for free school meals and a bus pass
- Apply for help from social services for elderly dependants and get information about day care centres
- Register a complaint about anti-social behaviour or faulty streetlights
- Pay their rent

Before CRM was introduced and the new customer service centres opened, in order to access this range of services the same person would have had to visit seven different receptions at the Civic, one at a different council office, phone up about other enquiries and visit one external agency.

can look that up for them and put them in the right direction, then you do.'

In the process of setting up customer service centres, targets were set – but were altered in line with the changing needs of customers and the kinds of services that were being provided. The initial target for customer service centres was to see 95 per cent of all customers within a waiting time of five minutes, but this was relaxed to 85 per cent to allow enquiries to be dealt with fully.

In particular, it was found that some of the new services available from the front desk of customer service centres were taking longer than anticipated. The issuing of 'blue badge' disabled parking permits, for example, can take up to 30 minutes. This is because previously application forms and accompanying documents such as proof of identity were passed to the parking control department of the council for processing, rather than being dealt with on the spot.

## Better access for most is not always better access for all

The transformation of council services, and in particular the centralisation of services following the closure of neighbourhood housing offices, has left some people, particularly the elderly and those on benefits, feeling they have a less personalised service.

Some benefits staff at the council say that when they were permanently based in local housing offices, they had more familiarity with customers. They often oversaw a claim through from start to finish – and were thanked afterwards. There was a dip in the speed of dealing with new claims and changes in circumstances just after the new systems went live but recent figures indicate that turnaround times are now at their most rapid levels ever and are among the quickest in the country. Some of the savings from the closure of neighbourhood housing offices have also been channelled into the creation of frontline visiting teams to help the housebound.

Dee Johnson is an advice worker for the Search Project, which helps elderly people in one of the city's poorest neighbourhoods: not Benwell in the west end of the city. This part of the city was one of the last places to have a customer service centre. It was opened in November 2008. Until then there was a housing office but, says Dee, ' it was wasn't welcoming at all, the counters were very high, you had to discuss your benefit problems publicly unless you made a special request which a lot of elderly people don't like to do and there were no public toilets'. What do staff and the elderly people they work think of the new centre? 'It's too soon to tell for certain', says Maggie Crane, Dee's co -worker who had a special affection for the Benwell library which has moved from its old and much used building, to into the purpose built customer service centre, ' but it looks good, with nice seating, private interview rooms, public toilets and a welcoming manager.' The staff from the library and the customer service staff seem to have made sure that it is user friendly, carrying over the best traditions of the old library.

Sarah Smart of the Rights Project, also in the inner west end of the city, says that some of those who come to her project are very poor and without a landline and cannot afford to phone the contact centre. ' Some of the East European immigrants who are using our project earn under £100 a week and have a family to support . Some can't even afford mobiles so they come to us,' she says. 'The new customer service centre has eased the problem but if you can't afford the bus fare, it's a long walk.' She continues: 'And there are people with disabilities and the elderly who can't always get there. We' re here to fill the gap.' As an afterthought, she suggests that maybe the council could, ' re-imburse us, especially where interpreting costs are involved.' Sarah is positive though about how the council deals with the enquries from the refugees and immigrants who use the Rights project. 'I would say that the people there certainly put themselves out,' Sarah says. 'I haven't had any complaints from colleagues here that they feel they've been fobbed off by anyone.'

## Un-joined up services

The fragmentary nature of public service provision as a result of privatisation of some services (for example buses) has also created problems. When the Kenton customer service centre opened in 2005, a bus route, operated by Stagecoach, served local people in neighbouring districts. That route has since closed, with the result that people from those areas have to catch two buses or take a taxi to access the centre. This adds to concern over the accessibility of public services that are increasingly being consolidated and moved to a limited number of joint-service locations. It's a problem that the council is trying to resolve with Stagecoach.

An additional problem arises from the fact that four of Newcastle's six customer service centres were funded under the Private Finance Initiative (PFI) LIFT programme, which is aimed at bringing together different services under one roof and involves a partnership between a private company, a company part owned by the Dept of Health and part by a private company, Newcastle City Council and two PCTs. The private company has three board members and the public bodies one between them. The fact that it is a PFI scheme, inherited rather than initiated by City Service, and not under the control of the Council has made it difficult for City Service's commitment to full and effective consultations with local residents about the Customer Service Centres always to be carried through in relation to decisions concerning the buildings at which these four centres are based.[1]

Customer services staff, non-specialists, who are the first point of contact for users of the customer service centres, must also link up service users with public agencies that are not part of Newcastle Council. Your Homes Newcastle (YHN), for example, a non-council organisation, is now responsible for the city's council house tenants. The connection is not always seemless however. 'The staff at our customer service centre are Newcastle City Council staff and if you are asking a questions about Your Homes Newcastle, they don't always know the answer,' says Margaret O'Callaghan who chairs the Outer West Community Forum, which advises the council. YHN reply that it 'always has staff available at the Outer West customer service to resolve problems too specialist for customer service staff'.

Margaret has also found that some of the older people with whom the Forum is in contact do not like the CRM computer system and would prefer face-to-face contact with decision-makers, even though CRM can make transactions quicker and simpler and someone is working on the computer for you. They tell her: 'They want to get past that computer and speak to the person making decisions' she says. A problem to be fed back to the script writers perhaps or, as Margaret suggests, for someone from City Service to meet the older people she works with and discuss how the CRM system can work better for them.'

## The response so far

Despite these real problems for some council service users, most notably the elderly, most people seem impressed with what has been achieved so far by City Service.

According to the national one-stop shop benchmark survey run by Sheffield Hallam University, which surveys customer opinions of local authority 'one-stop shops', the people of Newcastle are very satisfied with the service they receive from customer service centres. They give the centres a 95 per cent satisfaction rating.

What of flesh and blood reactions? Some anecdotal

evidence suggests that City Service's attempt to introduce a customer-centred philosophy to the services it provides has worked. 'At the present time, 99 times out of 100, they sort out your problem,' says Bill Bowman, a pensioner from Newcastle's Denton district. 'It's very rare when they can't help you.' Audrey Shakespeare, who at the beginning of this chapter described some of the frustrations of dealing with the old system, says services have 'vastly improved ... You can get to the people you need to be put through to and you can get your problems sorted out pretty quickly – both face to face and on the phone.'

## Much more than a technological fix

A whole chain of relationships is involved in improving quality and reducing costs. A central dynamic in the Newcastle transformation programme was the move from a technology chosen and configured to suit 'the way things have always been done' to technologies customised to help improve services and reduce costs. There are still improvements to be made and the staff and management know that. Their ability to keep on improving depends in good part on how creatively focused each section of City Service is on the end goal of a constantly evolving and responsive service to the public.

It is revealing, therefore, to go behind the scenes to room 213 – a vast open plan room in the Civic – and talk to the people involved in choosing the CRM technology for Newcastle Council. Neil Glendinning and Ron Hillaby were key contributors to the decisions about who should supply the CRM system and how it would be configured to respond to the varied and often complex needs of individual citizens. They are colleagues in the application services section of the ICT division of which Ron Hillaby is one of the senior managers. 'We look after ... the technological systems for payroll, for revenues and benefits, for the general ledger, purchase ledger, the systems which underpin the provision of neighbourhood services – that is, the practical services like roads and street cleaning – and the customer service system, the CRM,' explains Ron.

The crucial decision about Newcastle's CRM system was not taken on the basis of a socially neutral notion of technical prowess. Rather the criteria also included the flexibility to respond to the council's public need-oriented priorities. 'Some companies were offering a CRM package which effectively dictated to us the point where the system (of navigating through council departments) stopped and handed the user to a departmental specialist,' says Neil Glendinning disapprovingly. 'What we needed was a package which takes account of the variations and also leaves some discretion with the staff and the script writers.' The point at which it usually proves necessary for the script and the system to suggest going to a specialist is much earlier in the search for a solution to a social work problem, for example, than a problem of waste collection.

The decision was made to choose Lagan, a relatively small company based in Northern Ireland, which since 2000 has been developing CRM specifically for the public sector. 'They were sensitive in their approach and keen to collaborate,' says Neil Glendinning.

Predictably, perhaps, Dave Chapman from Lagan is enthusiastic about the potential of CRM for the public sector. But he echoes the City Service approach of taking innovations from the private sector and adapting them to meet public service needs. 'CRM initially was about increasing customer loyalty and identifying how to extract further profits from an individual. We're developing the software so that it provides all the information to enable users of council services to solve problems there and then.' He welcomes the opportunity he and other Lagan staff had to collaborate with City Service, joining workshops with council staff at every level from frontline services to Ron Hillaby, Neil Glendinning and others from the technology side. It's another example of working with the private sector on terms set by the public.

### Integrating the changes

In the case of CRM and the new system introduced for council tax (SX3), integration became a mega problem. The two systems had to talk to each other. Enquiries about council tax were one of the most common issues that customer service and contact centre staff had to deal with. To respond they needed detailed information about the state of people's council tax bills. To get into the council tax data CRM had to be integrated with the SX3 system by which council tax information was organised. Newcastle was one of the first councils to use CRM and going through many of such processes for the first time. In many respects it was going into the unknown.

Helen Batey, manager of the customer service section, takes up the story: 'When the council tax changed over to what they call SX3, we found out that it wasn't compatible with CRM and that was an absolute nightmare.' Ron Hillaby and his team moved into top gear, not only internally on Newcastle City Council but being a founding member of an 'adapters club' of other local authorities who were trying to integrate CRM with their council tax system. The gravity of the problem proved a bonding experience.

Word has it (he would not say so himself) that Ron Hillaby came up with the solution. At any rate, the adapters club produced a mechanism for integration. Then it was a matter of applying the integration software and testing and retesting it until it worked together with the CRM software without a flaw.

'We couldn't afford anything to be wrong from the back office because here we are talking about people's bills and income. And that is why the staff were so determined to make sure everything was sorted before it went live.' Helen Batey was proud of the role of the staff in this process. 'We said that until the frontline staff are happy, we are not going to give the go ahead. We would plead with them saying "Are you sure it is not ready?" and they said "No, no", and we said "You're not being too over cautious?" and they said "No, no." They were really committed.' And when it went live it was a success.

This story illustrates a lot – most obviously the advantages of genuine staff engagement, involving real decision-making power. Helen Batey again: 'It's been our philosophy at customer services that if you engage the staff, as well as the community, all the way along the change, you'll get a much more efficient service for the community.'

If a private company had been at the helm, moreover, there would undoubtedly have been greatly increased costs, with the company saying 'This wasn't part of the contract, it's additional – we have to charge you more.' Because the process was in-house, the solution could be found through collaboration with other local authorities and frontline staff , involving no extra costs other than increased staff time. Such collaboration would be difficult with the private sector in the lead.

## PART TWO: THE BACK OFFICE – SNAKES IN THE DARK

'Back office', 'BO', 'the bowels of the system'. When it comes to all the financial and administrative systems that keep the council going, the message to the average member of the public – and politicians – is: don't go there! A presumption that there is only one, technically determined, way of carrying out these bureaucratic functions and only the experts know what it is, together with a hefty dose of complacency, has traditionally meant that politicians rarely asked questions. The efficiency of the processes involved in, for example, chasing those owing money to the council or paying the invoices owed to suppliers, or meeting the council's salaries and pension payments to staff, was not scrutinised in a consistent way across departments. And snakes thrive in the dark. This low status of the back office and the sense that there are no social or political decisions involved in running it, made handing it over to a private company an attractive option for politicians.

In Newcastle, though, as the process of creating City Service dissolved departmental walls, costs were reduced and services improved without outsourcing to the private sector.

Self-scrutiny and a collaborative, cross-directorate focus on the council's responsibility for public funds made this possible. 'It's public money, so I felt we had a duty to look at the way we did things in order to maximise our use of resources. It's not like a frontline service, emptying bins or maintaining street lights – you have to create internal systems of accountability,' says Viv Hogg, the project manager who led the team for the unsexy-sounding project of 'process improvement and rationalisation'. (Basically this meant finding ways of dealing with bills more efficiently, standardising procedures for invoices, automating where possible, making debt collection speedier and more efficient in terms of the best use of people's time.) The target savings for the transformation of these transactions was £40,000 (the equivalent of two full-time staff). Responsibility for finding it lay with exchequer services, generally referred to as the 'exchequer'.

## Gold dust in the bowels

Working from a vast open-plan office in room 505 at the civic centre, the exchequer always had a close relationship with the treasury, the finance department down on the first floor. While the treasury's responsibility involves drawing up the council budget and ensuring the legal rectitude of its finances, the exchequer processes the money in and out.

Because the transformation programme flowed through and across departmental boundaries, Steve Evans, who led the changes in the exchequer, and Kevin Laing, head of financial systems and controls, were able to build up a strong working relationship, through which – with council treasurer Paul Woods – they managed to bring in an extra £1.7 million in revenues to the council. They accomplished this by getting the different directorates to speed up the recovery of debts, so improving the council's cash flow and adding to its income from investments.

The three of them made a powerful team and they systematically visited all five directorates – social services, education, neighbourhood services, planning and the chief executive's office – armed with an analysis of how each was managing its debt, identifying undue delays and indicating how systems could be standardised across directorates. They had a detailed agenda and scripted points about how each directorate could change the system to make it more alert to delays. In the past, for example, income was credited to department accounts as soon as an invoice was sent out; in future it would only be credited when the money actually came in.

'It was quite sensitive; we didn't want to come across heavy,' remembers Kevin Laing. 'So we put it in terms of "How can we help you?"' They also showed how the directorates' services would benefit from the increased efficiencies on debt collection. In particular, the increased income from interest would be reinvested in their services or used to soften the blow of government cuts.

Given the benefits of speeding up debt collection, why wasn't it done before?

'There's been a numbness to cash-flow issues in the council,' observes Steve Evans, 'mainly because each directorate runs its own budget in relative isolation from the position of the council as a whole. Also,' he adds, 'a lot of the debts are from public bodies. Directorates know they'll be paid eventually, so time isn't an issue from the point of view of their budgets in isolation from the council as whole.'

Part of Steve Evans' task, together with his two colleagues from the Treasury, therefore, involved cajoling the five directorates to think beyond their own budgets and to establish collaboration and accountability across the council. This is an example of how the changes allowed council staff to break out of their individual 'castles', or domains of work, and gain a wider view of how the whole range of services was working together.

This is such a clear case of significant savings being achieved through turning around the traditional culture and organisation of the council that it's worth looking at what happened in a little more detail.

## Working together to increase revenue

After Steve Evans' and Kevin Laing's shake-up trip round the directorates, a series of meetings was held with staff from these different services to discuss existing practices, highlight models that could be generalised, identify inefficient and sometimes hidden arrangements and begin the process of agreeing a standardised procedure. It wasn't easy. 'There was initially a prickliness at the idea of us coming to a meeting and telling people how they worked,' says Steve Evans. 'Too many people were thinking, "How will it affect me?" not "How do we work together to improve revenue to the council?"' says David Mitchell, one of the leaders of the process.

The next step involved 'focus groups' bringing together staff from all relevant areas to work together on the standardised system of income management and to purchase a technology package that would help run it. The groups, which met over a two-month period, involved a frontline member of staff and a finance person from each of the directorates along with several IT personnel who would be supporting the system.

'People found the approach refreshing in both the range of people brought together and the fact that it was very determined, structured, planned and minuted. It was accountable,' says David Mitchell. 'It was very much a consultation process. As well as the focus groups, there were the 'workstream teams.'

These involved everyone doing the work, from every level. They were very open; people could ask any questions. UNISON reps would encourage people to come forward with their questions. By all accounts, the managers leading the transformation really listened to the people doing the jobs. And the frontline people came up with ideas for improvement. 'There was a lot of trust; a very good relation with UNISON,' says David Mitchell. The result was substantial savings – in this case primarily through an improved revenue flow – well beyond the City Service targets.

## The advantages of doing it in public

All those involved emphasise how difficult it would have been to improve the efficiency of the council's debt management if the work had been outsourced. The recurring theme is that although breaking down departmental defences and disturbing people's comfort zones was difficult, it was worth it. The new relationships across the council, and the possibility of building on a shared commitment to the council's social goals, were a vital resource in creating a new collaborative culture.

According to David Mitchell, 'The advantage with being in-house was that we knew everybody. Everyone was fully aware of the objectives of the changes and shared the same commitment to the public. Of course, we would have co-operated whoever it was and maybe it would have been quicker but I don't think so much could have been achieved.'

Viv Hogg, who was responsible for improving the efficiency of bill payments, emphasises the energetic dynamic that was built on these relationships. Of course old relationships can reinforce inertia, she says, but 'there was a lot more engagement of all those affected, sharing ideas about how to improve things. People felt valued. Rather than having things done to them they had a say in their own destiny. The unions were visionary too in the support they gave. The result was that people were much more willing to come forward with their ideas. I don't think any of that would have happened with an outside company.'

When one considers what was involved in producing these efficiencies across the different directorates it is clear how important trust must have been – not as a passive quality but as the basis for active involvement. In its bare essentials the process was quite an astringent one, getting the directorates to come out of their nests, analyse and share how they managed their income, and agree on a standardised process – and then getting them to adopt this process as their own and take responsibility for implementing it.

They would then account to the powerful 'business management group' chaired by Barry Rowland. This was the key mechanism for ensuring that the different directorates became collaborators. At every point things could have broken down – and nearly did. A contract with a private company wouldn't have provided the time, flexibility and trust that were essential.

'There's so much that couldn't have been predicted in drawing up a contract. The company would either be trying to impose changes in a rush, which would have been unsustainable, or constantly negotiating changes, which would be very expensive,' says Kevin Laing from the treasury.

Based on his experience of speeding up the debt collection process, he adds two other conditions that it would have been difficult to achieve if a private company was in the lead role: 'We can be much more open and honest and also creative with each other than with a contractor. That was crucial to the success of my working relationship with Steve [Evans]. We worked really well together to get these changes. If we'd gone down the joint venture path with BT, I'd have had to be monitoring the contract with whoever was in his post, renegotiating anything that needed a change. It could never have worked as well as it did.'

Additionally, Kevin Laing says, 'As the council, we have a way of dealing with institutions who pay for our services (for example, businesses wanting pest control or new 'wheely bins') and owe us money that is not available to an external company. This also applies to collecting the council tax, where we can be much more flexible in response to social needs and hardship and leave more to the collector's discretion than a private contractor can.'

### Drilling for knowledge, discovering change
From Margaret Thatcher onwards, the orthodoxy of public sector change has been that the challenge of competition

from the private sector is a necessary stimulant, even if the end result is carried out internally. What is rarely given prominence is the idea of internal challenge, self-scrutiny and systematic questioning of the way things have always been done and the conditions that make it possible.

The demands of the City Service transformation process kickstarted in Newcastle a challenge to the way things had been done for the past 20 years or more. This process of drilling down into and breaking up accumulated layers of dusty habits in order to analyse and improve them was central to Steve Evans' method of achieving change. It became part of the City Service culture.

Steve Evans' shock at the inadequacy of management information when he arrived in Newcastle was just one aspect of the 'numbness' he observed. The kind of information he wanted to guide the transformation process required a lot more than the surface figures that normally pass for management information – staff numbers, absence statistics, performance against targets, costs and so on. His first step in transforming any of the exchequer services was to carry out what was effectively an investigation of every function, drilling down into all the processes and relationships through which it worked – or, more often, didn't work.

Take the payment of bills to suppliers. In what form did the bills come to the exchequer from the directorates? Was there anything wrong with the paperwork coming from the department that bought the service? Were the forms that the exchequer sent to the directorates to get the information flawed or confused in any way? How many stages were involved in the process? How could it be simplified and automated? Could more of the work be given to the bank? Could the way the supplier billed the council be simplified?

The questioning was always collaborative, through focus or 'diagonal' groups involving staff from every part of a process, whether it was paying bills or collecting debts – including, as we have seen, users or customers of exchequer services. The detailed questioning, going from level to level, was repeated for every function, leading directly to savings of time and to people doing more useful work.

Another good example of the efficacy of this process can be found in its application to the council's payroll services. It turned out that there were errors in 0.23 per cent of payroll payments to staff – almost one in every 500 payments. A considerable amount of time was being spent correcting errors that could be avoided at source. That information led to further questions. Was it the result of errors by the exchequer or in the information it was receiving? If the latter, could the forms be improved, giving the departments a better steer?

Some of the solutions coming out of this process were, looking in from the outside, so obvious that you have to ask why they weren't done before. Why were there hundreds of paper bills, one for every council landline, one for every council mobile, instead of a single electronic bill? And why weren't utility bills handled with a similar single bill or direct debit solution?

'Everyone just worked in their own areas. Now we have come together it's much clearer,' answers Viv Hogg. 'We lack a training in questioning and testing the best way of doing things,' says Steve Evans. 'The important thing,' he argues, 'is to understand the business in depth.'

Steve Evans stresses that this understanding should include how it relates to the goals of the council and other departments pursuing those goals. He makes a comparison – and contrast – with the private sector: 'There people would be much more aware of the bottom line, of how the business works. The public sector is a different business but it is still important that people know their business ... they should know the basic figures.' As with the private sector, there is a 'bottom line' in the City Service transformation. But instead of shareholder profit, it is maximising the efficiency of the back office functions so that resources can go to frontline services at the same time as ensuring that the back office is actively helping and linked to the front.

The process of collaborative questioning and understanding is creative and produces solutions that may not be possible in a private-sector context. The relationships built across departments and the sense of common purpose that such questioning creates is part of the solution. City Service's adoption of Gandhi's dictum 'Be the change you want to see in the world' is not just a trendy gesture.

## De-layering – the yeast in the transformation

One of the solutions arrived at in the exchequer and across City Service as a whole was 'de-layering': eliminating several supervisory roles. This was just one part of a reorganisation that also involved redefining managers' jobs. The new management job definitions emphasised their supportive, 'coaching' role, creating the conditions for frontline staff to do their jobs to the best of their capacity.

De-layering also involved enlarging the scope for initiative in many frontline jobs and in some cases increasing their number – in the new customer service centres and in the benefits section, for example. Steve Evans contrasts this with the habits of the past, more prevalent in some departments than others: 'Previous ways of adapting to problems had protected the senior managers and got rid of those at the bottom of the heirarchy'

The new approach had many benefits, which after the initial pain and disturbance of reorganisation showed themselves in sustained savings that were a result of more efficient methods, rather than cutting jobs and intensifying the work of those who remained. Often new jobs were created. The old systems had not just cossetted management but had hidden and sidelined talent elsewhere.

The yeast in the City Service transformation was people, mainly women as it happens, whose leadership talents were discovered during their contributions to the focus groups and other processes of change. They include Viv Hogg, who led the work on bills and debts; Paula Saul, who led the changes in the administration of payroll and human resources; Lisa Marshall in benefits; Andy Hopper on the IT side of benefits; Lisa Clark as an all-round project manager on the core transformation team. And so on.

The breakdown of hierarchies, and the mentalities that underpinned them, also opened up a horizontal, collaborative approach to solving problems. This was a driving feature of the transformation itself.

## PART THREE: A LADDER, BUT NOT OF THE CONVENTIONAL KIND

### Codifying the higgeledy piggedly

An exemplary case of focused collaboration was in the transfer of all the payroll, training and personnel or human resources information from the old mainframe computer set-up to the new system and the reorganisation of the work that went with it. The process was known, somewhat cryptically, as 'the SAP project' after the German company that supplied the technology. It was one of the most complex and sensitive projects in the transformation process, involving the transfer of data about pay, pensions, hours, training and so on – about 50 different recurrent activities in all – for 15,000 staff.

This massive task proved a huge hurdle, and the first attempt to clear it – in 2001, before the creation of City Service – failed. City Service managers put this failure down to the lack of a focused team whose sole job was to deliver this new system ready for use in the new HR and payroll department. For the staff responsible at the time, the work had been one task among many.

The process of transfer wasn't a mechanical task. It involved delving into the policy assumptions, often implicit and informal, underlying the information, as well as the 'higgledy-piggledy' character, as the project leader Jeff Pasternack described it, of the information itself. This was the product of the wide range of informal and directorate-specific agreements, resulting from each of the different directorates having its own payroll and human resources set-up. The project group then had to work on a vision of how the information *should* be organised and processed to meet the needs of all those who used or would be using it – the different directorates, the unions, individual staff and so on.

In this way the equivalent of the deep investigation that Steve Evans carried out for the exchequer was carried out in the information transfer from the old mainframe computer to the new system. It took place through critically mapping the rules that underlay the existing information on the mainframe, followed by envisioning – within the framework of council-wide industrial relations and human resources policies – what information was needed for the new system and how it should be organised.

'You can't simply put in the new technology, you need to think through new ways the service has to be organised, new processes and relationships, different skill levels, and how you're going to get there,' says Julia Woollard, who as programme manager had to be alert to any signs of projects that were going awry. One aim was to systematise and centralise the information, making it easier for all to access and use and more efficient to process.

## A dedicated project team
Each of these tasks, analysing the business as it was and envisioning how it should be, could be done well only if carried out collaboratively by a team of people with an intimate understanding of the tasks under discussion.

Each needed the concentrated input of the people who produced and used the information and of those who processed it – the different directorates on the one hand and the payroll and human resources specialists on the other.

It was also important for the efficiency of the new processes that those who collaborated on this mapping and envisioning worked on the frontline of these services and could contribute practical knowledge.

'They gave me a 100 per cent dedicated team. We had to imagine all the scenarios,' says Jeff Pasternack, the energetic, bureaucracy-busting project team leader. 'Part-time jobs, multiple jobs, putting people into two jobs, then one of the jobs is taken away – we had to understand these scenarios end to end, asking what is the form that triggers each scenario? And how do we rationalise the number of forms coming into human resources or payroll? Then what do you do in the system, then what do you do about verification letters? So it was trying to create an end-to-end business process.'

The project team of 15 was made up of staff central to both payroll and human resources who had experience in different directorates. They worked alongside five IT technicians from Pecaso, the company that had procured the SAP system for City Service and was responsible for configuring the new system as the rest of the team required. Jeff Pasternack was himself an experienced manager of IT systems.

The choice of Jeff Pasternack to lead and deliver the project and the terms on which he worked, is another illustration of City Service culture in action. The initial plan for the SAP project had been to ask Fujitsu to bring in one of its high flyers. But when Pasternack applied for the job as manager of exchequer services, to which Steve Evans was appointed, Kath Moore, who headed the transformation and development team (explained in chapter 3), recognised Pasternack's evident ability and commitment and employed him to lead project delivery – at two thirds of what it would have cost to have done it through Fujitsu. Here was Kath Moore's ability as a 'people picker' at work, backed up by City Service director Ray Ward's willingness to be flexible.

Jeff Pasternack's brief was tight. 'I signed in blood with the council that I would hit the time deadline of 18 months with the [savings target] of £1.6 million,' he recalls with a grin. Both he and his team were under particular pressure to succeed. It was the first and most exposed project in the transformation process.

## Autonomy and accountability

Partly in response to the previous failure, another important feature of the SAP project team was the nature of its autonomy and accountability in relation to City Service and to the council. This combination of autonomy – strongly protected and supported by Kath Moore's transformation and development team – and accountability through a simple and transparent reporting system to City Service's programme board was a key feature of the City Service approach, and one of the conditions of its success.

In the case of the payroll/SAP team, the autonomy was physical as well as organisational, much to Jeff Pasternack's delight (he's not a corporate character). In his words, 'The nicest, smartest thing they did – I don't know if it was by chance or not – was to give us a town house over there.' He was pointing out of a window at the back of the civic centre to a location near the Friends Meeting House in Jesmond, a well-appointed neighbourhood of Newcastle.

'We had a mini sub-culture. The fluorescent lights were turned off and we got iridescent lights. We played music whenever we wanted. If anybody wanted to have a meeting at Starbucks, that was fine. People were free to come in at five in the morning and they could leave at one in the afternoon as long as they understood that every day at 9am we had a 20-minute meeting quickly round the table – what are we doing? what's the programme? who's doing what? – so that communication was absolutely fluid and easy. A "nine o'clock", we called it – they hated me for it!'

They needed it, though, because the project timetable and budget was more Germany than California. As a result, Pasternack was determined to keep his team of 15 absolutely focused and he made sure they weren't pulled into meetings at the Civic five minutes away. 'We tried to keep the town house pure. They knew what they had to deliver, but it was up to us how we did it. We gave people complete responsibility for a module – payroll, pension, performance and appraisal, and so on. But people were very supportive of each other, willing to move off one exercise into another to support somebody. At times we lived the project.'

The input of the unions was important too. Tony Carr, the UNISON rep seconded to full-time union work on the transformation process, played a role in the 'vision' group. 'Tony was all over the project,' remembers Jeff talking about the transformation programme as a whole, 'if only from sheer interest in it. He was happy in his role.'

A lot of the issues concerned the union. Its officers could see the advantages of codifying and then rationalising the 'higgledy-piggledy', especially since, in the words of one member of the team, Paula Saul, 'when we mapped all the existing processes, we identified best practice so that we could capture it and spread it through the new system. Also there was a lot of informality, which didn't live up to employment law.'

There had to be relationships with the civic centre, though, especially room 505. This was where the everyday business of the human resources and payroll section of City Service was based, alongside the other exchequer services whose transformation we described earlier – all under the supportive leadership of Steve Evans.

Jeff Pasternack's relationship to Steve Evans as head of the exchequer was crucial to his ability to deliver. While Jeff was responsible for delivering a system fit for use, configured to take account of the needs of all its customers and users, Steve was responsible for deploying this new system across the exchequer, with all the reorganisation of the department and the change in culture and ways of working that this would imply.

This included changing people's jobs (indeed, changing the whole job structure), retraining, losing jobs, redeployment, cutting out layers of supervision, developing work teams to give staff scope to take the initiative and bear more responsibility. The timetable for transferring the data and configuring the technology, on the one hand, and preparing the staff and the organisation of the exchequer to carry on paying the salaries, monitoring absenteeism, organising pensions, supporting training and so on had to be in sync. The understanding was that there should be 'no unpleasant surprises'.

In the event, the discipline of Jeff Pasternack's 'nine o'clocks' delivered the new system in time for the three-phase introduction that Steve Evans and Ray Ward had planned. The creative atmosphere of the Jesmond town house also made sure that the content of the new system had some innovations that were a pleasant surprise.

## PART FOUR: REVS AND BENS – SNAKES AND (EVENTUALLY) LADDERS

If any individual service or cluster of services was closest to a game of snakes and ladders it was 'revs and bens', revenues and benefits – especially 'bens' – and, by all accounts, it wasn't fun. Talk to any group of benefits staff in 2008 after they'd been in the game since 1999 and they'd tell you what they'd been through with the slightly frenetic energy of a group of people who'd just emerged from a disaster zone.

Their experience started in 1999/2000 with 'verification', a process encouraged by the government whereby benefit claimants would have to verify their identity with two means of identification rather than the customary one. It wasn't compulsory but the government was offering money to those councils that did it. Staff complain that no one consulted those who had to implement it and cope with the inevitable backlog, nor the claimants who had to submit to it and face the ensuing delays to their claims, with all the knock-on effects this had in terms of rent arrears and so on. It was a significant, slippery snake.

Not long after verification came centralisation. In 2003-2004, synchronised with the opening of the new customer service centres, the council's benefits staff were all moved from the 22 neighbourhood offices to the old Scottish Life Insurance House, five minutes walk from the civic centre. 'Moved' was the operative word. Again staff say that the process was done to them, disregardful of their long experience and extensive practical knowledge.

Looking back, the staff can see the arguments for the change, especially in the context of the new customer service centres. But, they say, no one discussed it with them. There were no job losses but the move radically changed the daily lives of all of them. Moreover, they felt they could have suggested ways of improving the transformation process from the point of view of the claimants they knew so well, as well as from their own experience. Another snake.

Then, in 2003 came the first move towards the new technology – the first impact of the City Service transformation process. This was the shift from working from paper claim forms, and keying in the information manually, to having the forms scanned and then processing them electronically.

The procurement of this document management system, like most of the new systems associated with the transformation programme, was in the hands of Fujitsu. Under the guaranteed maximum price contract that City Service had negotiated (see chapter 7), Fujitsu bore all the financial risk if anything went wrong. It was an early purchase in the transformation programme. The procurement process went through the newly established process of comparing alternative systems against agreed criteria with a cross section of the staff who would be operating or affected by it, visiting places where the system was in operation and subjecting Fujitsu's procurement recommendation to a 'challenge' meeting chaired by Ray Ward.

Nevertheless, it became apparent as it was being implemented that it was the wrong choice for Newcastle. Instead of being a source of savings and a way of speeding up the processing of benefit claims, it was the cause of delays, frustration and wasted time. This one was a bit of a python.

The next step in the move to the new technology went relatively smoothly. This was the vital process of shifting the whole of benefit processing from the old mainframe computer to the new SX3 system, widely used by other councils. It was worked on by SX3 (now Northgate), the company that had developed the system, in close collaboration with government agencies, to change procedures automatically in response to every relevant change in government legislation. There were six weeks of downtime during the transition, while the information was transferred from the old system to the new one, but something of this order had been expected and detailed plans had been put in place.

Potentially, the new system provided by Northgate gave the benefits staff more scope in the organisation of their work and enabled management to organise the workflow more smoothly, with the end result of reducing the time it took to process claims by up to half. It was brought in without the redundancies that people always fear with the introduction of any new technology but also without adequate end-to-end training – and, above all, without any change in how the whole department was managed. It was the first ladder in years but too short to make much difference, either to staff morale or to the efficiency of the process as it affected claimants. Looking back, staff talk about how 'there's been no structure to the work and we've had to bear the brunt of it'.

With no ladders in sight within the benefits section, Ray Ward and the City Service leadership took action and Steve Evans took the lead. A new document management system was procured with the full involvement of the staff who used it (and who now had a much better understanding of what Newcastle needed). The scanning of benefit applications was taken back in-house from the company to which it had been contracted, to the dismay of staff, in Rotherham. And after an extensive process of consultation a very different organisational structure was developed, which pushed initiative and management closer to the frontline, linked the benefits staff much more closely with the customer service centres and the contact centre and broke down divisions between the front and back office.

By early 2008, benefits staff were beginning to have a sense of purpose and direction and, above all, a feeling that their work and abilities were being recognised. 'In the end, Steve Evans' changes were more for us than for management,' one of them comments. A big ladder was in place. But staff at that time felt they needed more support before they could climb it.

It was the most challenging part of the transformation process for the leadership of City Service and for UNISON. It was a part, too, that put the relationship between the union and the council to the test and proved the importance of them working together, both as a driver and a guarantor of change.

## Change is never easy

The reason why the transformation of 'revs and bens' was such a challenge went to the heart of the cultural and organisational problems with the old form of command management. The department was run by managers who were effective in delivering the service under the old technology and had no technical problem with moving to the new technology – indeed, they managed the technical-mechanical side of the transition with competence.

But they did not see the need for change in either how they managed or how the processing of benefits fitted in with other services to the public. And they argued with those such as Ray Ward, Steve Evans, Lisa Clark and the unions who told them that change was necessary.

A member of staff remembers the first meeting when the changes were announced to management: 'There were probably about 20 people. It was all the great and good from customer services, all the great and good from revenues and benefits. It was very tense. A lot of positives came from customer services because they'd already gone through quite a lot of change, whereas revenues and benefits maintained that the systems in place were efficient and reliable.'

The reasons for the strength of feeling were clear. One participant comments: 'There wasn't an understanding of why anything had to change. They considered that were delivering a good service and why did anything have to change? There was a set of job losses there too. They didn't know whether they might lose their jobs.'

The memory of those months is a reminder that though City Service is a success story, some of its chapters have been difficult. Its leadership abjures tactics of fear but its strategy of support and the unions' commitment to all its members have at times both been stretched to their limits.

## Future focus

In order to overcome the fear and uncertainty, management used a technique known in management circles as the 'future operating model'. When Lisa Clark – responsible for the initial phases of the revs and bens transformation, as Jeff Pasternack was for the SAP project – explains it, it sounds more like common sense.

'We called it a future operating model because that's exactly what it was about,' she says. 'It was a way of getting people to focus on the future. We used a "diagonal" group of staff drawn from across different levels of the service. Our approach was to say we appreciate that you've done things differently historically but we need to focus on the future and on how we can deliver this service better to the customer. Over a period of months, we got them to draw up a set of design principles for the new organisation. The idea was that they would then own it and implement it. These were facilitated workshops. We didn't make any input.'

The group – ordinary staff as well as management – met over an eight-month period. Among other things it drew up an impressive list of ten principles – even if the English doesn't exactly trip off the tongue. They include such statements as:

- Staff will have a better understanding of how they fit in, how their individual actions impact the delivery of the end-to-end service and how they can positively influence customer satisfaction.
- This will improve customer service as all staff (irrespective of their role in the end-to-end process) will have shared aims and objectives.
- 'Problem passing' and transferring ownership of customer problems will be eliminated, as the customer's needs will become owned by the entire service.
- 'Silo thinking' will be eliminated.
- A cross-cutting view of service delivery will provide greater opportunity to plan the resources around the demands of the service i.e. it will enable better management of peaks and troughs and ensure complementary performance through service and support functions.

Clearly, some people in these diagonal groups understood the change that was necessary. The problem as far as the benefits section was to make sure that it happened.

## A radical plan
In the end, Ray Ward got Steve Evans to prepare for benefits (now part of Evans' remit as well as his responsibility

for the exchequer) a radical plan to tackle the structure and culture of management. To turn the plan or anything like it into reality was a very difficult process. The benefits section had been in a world of its own, with its need to respond more to government changes than council policies and with a certain craft and specialist consciousness. As we have seen, it had just been through a very destabilising process of radical change through the centralisation of the service and then the creation of a three-monthly rota of duties at customer service centres.

The benefits section management's way of dealing with the change was to allow little room for debate. It was management by command rather than involvement and collaboration. Steve Evans had the task of upturning this culture and the top-heavy structure that underpinned it. 'The way management had made savings was by not filling vacancies at the lowest level – effectively the frontline,' he says. As a result there was a heavy burden on frontline workers, who were afraid to complain, lest they lost their jobs.

Evans' proposal effectively involved a cull of senior management positions. It was nothing personal but a structural shift towards the kind of 'flat' arrangement built around teams dealing with specific tasks that he had and others had successfully implemented in the exchequer.

He developed the proposal after spending some time talking to staff at every level. He had established a certain credibility by ensuring that the original document management system was replaced through the procurement of a more appropriate one with the full involvement of a cross section of the staff. At the same time he brought the documents scanning system in-house – something that benefits officers were screaming for. And he worked through his proposals with UNISON.

On the issue of restructuring revs and bens, Kenny Bell, the UNISON branch secretary, was centrally involved. Lisa Marshall, the energetic and able trade union rep in benefits, was initially involved too. At the time she was an assistant senior benefits officer, a position between management and staff, and found her position contradictory and withdrew from being a rep. She wanted to be free to make criticisms of Steve Evans' plan. She did exactly this within the process of consultation negotiated between City Service and the unions, and achieved the amendments she wanted. But that is skipping the difficult bit.

Steve Evans announced his plans on 30 November 2006 to a meeting of management and staff. The aim was to implement it by March 2007. In fact it was completed on 4 June of that year – Lisa Marshall remembers the date exactly because from that point on she became a team leader dealing with quality control of the processing of claims. At the meeting, there were more tears and 'inappropriate language ... people don't like to remember it and I don't want to go through anything like it ever again,' she says firmly.

The plan effectively involved the elimination of a layer of senior management: six senior jobs. UNISON had signed up for change in management culture and structure, so Kenny Bell had no hesitation in supporting Steve Evans as long as there was a full and responsive consultation process. He knew that UNISON members in the benefits section wanted a change in management processes but found it difficult openly to press for it – senior management are members of UNISON too.

Kenny Bell explains how the unions 'knew that these resistances to change were around amongst senior management [but] this was a key part of the in-house bid. The problem was how to manage the transformation process. It was our reps who were saying, "Look, we love these people, they're very capable in the world. But are they able to lead a process of change?" There's a bit of a contradiction there, but we negotiated an approach about how we were going to manage job loss that applied to the senior managers as well.' Eventually the senior managers resigned as a group taking voluntary redundancy or redeployment.

Just as important as this aspect of the change was the positive modification of Steve Evans' plan that Lisa Marshall and others achieved through the extended consultation process. Lisa Marshall's concern – and that of many of her colleagues – was not with the move towards a flatter staffing structure in itself, pushing more scope for initiative to a lower level. The staff had been arguing for this as early as the first workshops on the in-house bid. The disagreement was over the staffing at a middle level.

The elimination of management levels carried with it the risk of losing a lot of knowledge and expertise built up from experience and leaving the frontline staff unsupported – something that would be contrary to the City Service strategy of management performing a role as supports and coaches. The assistant senior benefit officers – a layer that Steve Evans proposed be abolished – were no longer mainly assisting the senior benefits officers, as they had been in the neighbourhood offices, covering when they were absent, managing the administrative staff. The job had become a vital source of technical support in the centralised process.

'If you get rid of those posts, who does that work? It puts too much of a burden on the frontline and deprives the frontline of support they need,' said Lisa Marshall. More of these posts should be retained, she argued.

After a long process, she won her point. 'We ended up influencing it. Two scale sixes – the assistant benefit officer level – and two senior benefit officers were retained,' she says. Later Steve Evans decided to appoint a single manager beneath him to oversee and support the team leaders in revenues and benefits. 'A cracking idea,' says Lisa Marshall. 'They can pick up on more management issues than he can from his strategic position in City Service [where he also has overall responsibility for the exchequer and payroll sections].'

Looking back now, what does Lisa Marshall, who is once again becoming active in UNISON, think about the transformation process? 'I would have given up if it hadn't been for the consistency of the process,' she says. 'The restructure felt quite brutal and wrong in some respects. It was important that we could cling onto a clear and transparent process and common objective that staff, trade unions and management could all buy into and influence.'

She goes on to make a contrast with the past: 'Before it was very much conflict management. Managers would say this is the way we are moving forward on this service without any real consultation. Staff would say, well, we don't like that and they'd institute a grievance and the status quo would be maintained until those issues were thrashed out. Now it's very much that the managers will interact with the staff side and go through the staff before they implement changes, so that staff are quite on board with it and have influenced it.'

An important precondition for this was the negotiated framework for retraining, redeployment and support for those who did not have a job of their choice in City Service. The deal, remember, committed the council to avoiding compulsory redundancies.

1.  See the 'Evaluation of Benwell Library Building' by Knowledge Inclusion Project (KIP)

# Chapter 9

## The labour pains of change

The transformation promised by City Service was not just a question of changing the philosophy and practice of the council in the way it served the people of Newcastle. The success of the in-house bid also carried the responsibility of an internal restructuring and other changes that would deliver savings of £34.5 million over 11 and a half years. This cost-cutting commitment outshone BT's promises and was instrumental in securing political support for an alternative to outsourcing. In part, these savings would be achieved through IT systems such as Document Management System underpinning a new relationship with the users of council services, which would free up staff from routine tasks. But UNISON and the new management team also had to face up the unavoidable fact that an overwhelming part of the money they had promised to save the council would come through staff savings. There would be a human cost: people would lose their jobs.

The In-House option document had required that this shedding of jobs should be done be "humanely managed". Above all, there was a commitment to avoid compulsory redundancies, engage staff in the transformation process and provide opportunities for retraining and 'employment retention'. UNISON's position was that there must not be any compulsory redundancies. If this was to be honoured many staff would have to redeployed in different jobs within City Service and the Council as a whole. This was possible because as some parts of City Service contracted as part of the transformation, others were to grow. Alternatively, displaced workers might find positions elsewhere in the council or take voluntary redundancy.

The unenviable task facing City Service managers was to cull 153 posts, a quarter of the workforce of just over 600. But each post was a 'currency' rather than an actual job. In the benefits section, for example, 30 posts were to go and each post was worth £21,200. In payroll, a total of 25 posts were to be abolished and a single post was set at £16,400. This would lead to staff savings of 3.9m by March 2006, with the average lost post worth £25,400.

Human resources (HR) practices needed to be recast. Official council policy was to give staff a maximum of 12 weeks notice if they were to be made redundant. But Jackie Lowes, who was employed as an HR advisor working with City Service, says managers quickly realised that they had to go beyond legal obligations and existing policies. In many cases, the affected workers had been employed in the same job for 10-20 years. Most employers seek to avoid compulsory redundancies when shedding staff, but City Service realised more a proactive approach was required.

'I wouldn't say that 12 weeks is enough for anybody if they're going to have to think about taking a different [career] route or trying to do a different job,' says Lowes.

'So what City Service did was to engage with staff. They were being supported; it could be well in advance of a year before the change to their post. That gave people the right mindset, so they knew what they needed to do.'

City Service could not decide a year in advance which particular individuals would be made redundant. But the time span meant that the HR department could warn workers that job reductions were going to be made in their section and give them a chance to find alternative employment. Nor were the affected workers simply left to their own devices. 'Personally, I don't think it's enough just to say, "Look on the internet, here's a jobs bulletin,"' says Lowes. Those affected would be placed on the redeployment register and the HR department would alert them to newly available and suitable posts before they were advertised internally or externally. If they met the criteria, they would be offered preferential interviews, alongside other redeployed candidates, before a position was opened up to the rest of the council's staff.

Training was also an integral part of the package. Given many employees' length of service in the same job, that often meant help with job-hunting skills such as interview techniques, completing an application form or preparing a CV. Taster sessions were also offered enabling staff to spend a few days experiencing a job in a different part of the council.

Even so, none of this meant that redeployment was a simple process that matched staff seamlessly with alternative positions that perfectly reflected their skills and experience. It was not that painless. "A degree of stress and disturbance is almost inevitable," warned the in-house bid document prophetically.

David Moses, for example, a clerical and administrative worker in the housing benefit department, had worked for the council for 17 years. He says he was 'gobsmacked' when he was told in December 2005 that his contract would be terminated. Emailed jobs to apply for, he was successfully interviewed for a job with Newcastle's council-owned Discovery Museum. But the new job – a stocktaking role for the museum's shops – was very different to his previous post in housing benefit. 'There was so much extra knowledge that you had to take in,' he recalls. 'It wasn't like you could slot into it straightaway.' After 12 weeks, at a meeting with his line manager, union rep and HR advisor, Jackie Lowes, it was decided he was not suited to the position.

He then went for another interview and moved to the council's coin room, which counted and sorted the cash from the city's Metro system and parking meters. It was a very manual job. 'The process was so physical, I actually lost a stone and a half in a matter of two or three months,' Moses says. Twelve weeks in and he was called into another meeting and told that HR had found a position more suited to his skills – an admin job back within City Service. 'Eventually, redeployment worked for me, but I think it was a bit harsh in some ways,' says a reflective Moses. 'At the time, it was a very difficult period for me, but I'm resilient and I just got through it. But I wonder how somebody who wasn't so resilient would have felt.'

There was conflict in sections of the council that had no future in the transformed City Service. The cashiers, who worked in the neighbourhood housing offices and received housing benefit, rent and council tax payments, felt they provided an important community service, especially for isolated elderly people. But many local offices were closing as part of the transformation and they were told that some staff would be transferred to customer service centres, while others would not have their fixed-term contracts renewed. 'We wanted to know why, and what we had done, after being there for years, to suddenly feel worthless,' recalls one. But five of them were eventually redeployed within the council.

The print section also presented a challenge. Printing was carried out in the traditional fashion, typesetting documents and using plates and ink. It was decided at an early stage that this function would be not be retained in City Service, but no remotely similar job existed in any other part of the council.

'Now, plainly, those people were skilled in terms of those jobs, and there wasn't a chance of being redeployed in that sort of job elsewhere in the authority because we didn't have it anywhere else,' says Jackie Lowes. 'So what were we going to do with them?' Here City Service's proactive approach helped to pave the way to a solution. Print staff were told they were going to lose their job, but given 18 months to find alternative employment. In the event, two were re-trained in the digital printing service the council has set up to replace the old print section. Another was redeployed in an administrative job after a taster session and taking training packages in Word and Excel.

There were times when City Service did come close to compulsory redundancies. 'Sometimes, you had people who were under formal notice [of redundancy] and you're desperately trying to redeploy them because they don't want to go, and there were times when we've been right up against the wire,' says Margaret Clayton, the ex Unison branch official who City Service employed as the HR consultant on the Transformation and Development Team. 'And that's when you've got to be innovative.'

Staff who were within a few weeks of the end of their notice period were frequently found temporary work within another part of City Service. Sometimes those temporary jobs became permanent because City Service itself was creating work as well as rationalising posts. In 2006, the document management system, which scanned benefits documents, was brought back in-house following a failed out-sourcing to a firm in Rotherham. Six clerical staff who were losing their jobs were redeployed to work on the new in-house system.

Did the redeployment process deliver on its promise to be humane? Most feel satisfied with the outcome, even if the 'stress and disturbance' along the way was not a pleasant experience. "Eventually it worked out for me," says Moses. "But I did think it was a bit harsh in some ways and I must say, at the time, it was a very difficult period for me."

# Chapter 10

## Positively public, QED

This story should make policy makers and the media look at the public sector and local government with new eyes. Here is a summary of the evidence that City Service delivered improved services and made savings.

- Since the transformation process described in this book, people receiving housing and other welfare benefits in Newcastle receive them quicker than in most other major UK cities.[1]
- The percentage of benefits processed correctly is 98.4% (2nd amongst core cities)
- Phone queueing time for access to council services has fallen from around five minutes to around two minutes.
- In 2008 a survey of the new Contact Centre in the Civic showed 91% customer satisfaction and evidence that the new arrangements are reaching the people who need them - 30% of callers are ill, disabled or infirm.
- A survey of the Customer Service Centres in 2008 gave satisfaction levels of 95%. [2]

At the same time as delivering better services, City Services has achieved real savings:

- Newcastle council now collects more council tax and other revenue owed to it[3] than it did before.

- By 2007 the annual cost of administering the payroll per employee had fallen from £49 to £26. This is almost half the CIPFA benchmark average of £49.
- The costs of processing each benefit are now £10 below the average of major cities.

These and other reductions add up to £28 million net savings[4] over an 11 ½ year period.

## Why it matters beyond the banks of the Tyne

The government's new National Efficiency and Improvement Strategy of January 2008 sets goals of 'improving value for money; increasing innovative capacity; and community empowerment'.[5] City Service has reached them already - through a *public*-led transformation that improved the quality of its service, generated real savings, and expanded its activities and its employment.[6] And they have done so with the active involvement of the staff, not at the expense of staff.

For Lib-Dem Council leader John Shipley the lesson of City Service is that 'the public sector can organise itself efficiently and deliver self-improvement'.

## Real choice and personalisation

The City Service experience challenges the widespread belief that inefficiency is inherent in state 'monopoly' of public services. It demonstrates driving forces for change that are special to the public provision of public services. It shows that methods that mimic the private sector are neither necessary nor appropriate to creating public services responsive to the varied needs of individual citizens, communities and local organisations.

Newcastle council became more responsive through regular and direct consultation with service users and potential users, including surveys and extensive feedback, and training of frontline staff to help them be as sensitive as possible to the customers' wishes.[7] The result is a set of services that have an inbuilt capacity to monitor themselves, respond to complaints and improve.

Newcastle 's Customer Services now provide a more personalised service than similar services elsewhere that have been privatised. Where appropriate – for example mechanisms for council tax payment and rent – they introduced a wide range of options.[8]

## Real participation and empowerment

Critics of privatisation have long argued that 'democratisation' should drive change. This has generally meant strengthening citizens' involvement in control over the spending of taxpayers' money.[9,10] But what about the democratisation of the public management and administration of our public services? This has usually been limited to questions of accountability and scrutiny. But as long as the internal organisation of our local councils remains top-down, fragmented and semi-oblivious to the real potential of their staff, all the citizens participation in the world can be soaked up, defused or blocked by hierarchical structures and rigid bureaucratic procedures.[11]

What was exciting about the City Service experience was the opening up – by management and unions in tandem – of the dry-sounding, but actually vital, internal processes of managing public money. This created conditions for a thoroughgoing democratisation, from the policy commitment in the Council Chamber to the complex processes of implementation of policies in the delivery of frontline services. However, without the wider political campaign against privatisation there would not have been the political will to give this project the support it needed at the right time.

In Newcastle the union's mobilisation in support of the in-house bid gave management the confidence to make a success of it. The unions never intended it to be *their* in-house bid. They were always insistent that management should lead, in a close relationship with the unions whose positive engagement and organisational strength was a necessary condition for the success of the transformation.

## How did they get here from there? The things that made it work...

The transformation in Newcastle began with the threat, and virtual fait accompli, of outsourcing to BT. But we don't keep dropping apples in order to verify the laws of gravity, and councils need not go through the considerable expense of competitive tendering to understand and develop democratic mechanisms of change.[12] Although sensitivity to local variation and conditions is vital, if we understand the conditions which produced and favoured the changes reported here key relationships are replicable without repeating the experiment.

*People*
The focus on people, on encouraging them, supporting them, believing in them has been *systemic* to the transformation programme. Where possible, hierarchies were eliminated, also some supervisory layers, in order to push initiative back to the frontline, where it could be highly effective. An approach to leadership developed which was to do with support rather than control. In Ray Ward's words 'Relax, don't freeze - recognise the future is uncertain ... you don't become unbureaucratic bureaucratically'.

If this seems common sense, all too often, managers or consultants – in both the private and public sectors – draw up 'transformation plans' without much thought on involving, galvanising and supporting the people who will deliver the changes. Belief in the capacities and ingenuity of staff underpinned a collaborative, problem-solving approach.

A high priority was given to supporting people as they planned their future in response to the changes, giving them time, training, full support to find redeployment within the council, successfully avoiding compulsory redundancies.

*Common and clear vision and values*
City Service management and UNISON, supported by the politicians, both Labour and Lib Dem, shared a common vision of a transformed public authority with improved

services that could make savings and redistribute them to frontline services. Every aspect of the transformation programme was geared to and judged by that goal. 'Keep the message true and consistent,' insisted Ray Ward.[13]

This shared goal provided a basis for motivation and common purpose; a mutually accepted reference point and compass that avoided drift and help to overcome conflict. It enabled management and union leadership constantly to move the process forward. A clear common direction was a precondition also for a decentralised system of management in which staff at the frontline had considerable autonomy and responsibility.[14]

### A service ethic

The shared vision served to dust off and bring to the fore a public service ethic that normally lies dormant or reduced to a matter of formal rhetoric. The ethics of public service can be a lot more dynamic than the familiar formal, and often inanimate, features of public sector culture. An active thinking-through of public service ethics was valued and encouraged in all parts of City Service. This included the call centre and customer service centres; back office staff; council tax debt collectors; payroll staff; benefit processing staff; and IT support staff going out to community organisations.

### A strong union voice

There is now widespread talk of 'empowerment' or 'releasing creativity' with regard to public service workers, an approach that implies taking public service workers as well as users seriously, but there is scant recognition of the necessity of a well organised and democratic trade union for achieving that. Newcastle UNISON – a branch that has built up an active membership with a strategic commitment to public service reform – was a key and indispensable actor in the transformation. The union placed a high priority on communications, education, membership involvement and the development of a new generation of leaders. Negotiating time off for training for union members and staff played a crucial role. The union organised an extensive 'workplace learning' scheme. It organised and represented its members so that staff felt secure, and in some sense protected, as they took risks and contributed to changes that sometimes transformed their working lives.[15] Although management and unions worked together, the union could escalate an issue to a point of conflict if agreements, including those concerning employment conditions, were broken.

One of many indispensable ingredients in the Newcastle UNISON mix was research. Strategic advice from the Centre for Public Services played a key role in getting the in-house bid accepted. It showed how vital it is for union branches and councils to have access to strategic research, so that they can draw richly on others' experience rather than locally re-inventing the wheel ad infinitum.

*Autonomous driver of change*
The autonomy of Kath Moore's Business Development and Transformation Team from day-to-day business was essential. It meant her team could develop an overview,

clearing time for reflection and problem-solving. This kept the vision in focus and alive. The flexibility and collaborative internal relationships which happened in this team and throughout the process were something an outside contractor could never supply.

*Question everything - leave nothing secret*
One weakness of change driven by threat, change in an atmosphere of tension, is that people are scared of asking questions and sharing knowledge.

By contrast City Service built into its very being forces of contestation, including self-contestation. The process was considerably helped by its collaborative ethos which was possible only because staff felt relatively secure. One of many benefits of this insistent questioning was an unusual degree of transparency. This contributed to the democratic follow through and the genuine account-ability of public officials to elected councillors and the public.

*The changing boundaries between public and private sector*
The commitment to publicly-led public service reform shaped City Service's relationship with private companies.

From the beginning it was clear that City Service would need to buy in help – both in purchasing hard-ware and in the management of particular projects – to achieve savings on a tight timetable. Yet among the lead-ership of City Service there was a strong commitment to transferring knowledge and avoiding the sort of dependent relationships that leave the host body weaker even if specific tasks are accomplished. There was an energetic collective determination to take the most useful and efficient tools of business practice developed in the private sector and adapt or transform them for social goals and democratic accountability.

## The future for City Services...
The City Service leadership did not operate with a fixed notion of the public sector, but a developing one. One development currently being explored by Newcastle Council is sharing services with other public sector bodies to achieve the kind of economies of scale that large private corporations present as one of their special strengths. Given Newcastle's experience in radically transforming and improving public services, City Service staff are confident they could collectively share this know-how with other councils. And indeed UNISON is already beginning to do so.

## Making accountability a political reality
A strategy for public service reform based on the importance of democracy at all points in the process must address the problem of the UK's blunt electoral institutions. The elected assemblies of local government should surely be the trigger of change and an important monitor of its good working? I reported in chapter 1 how a leading councillor, looking back to the days of the mainframe computer and its constant adaptation, described how, 'there was always another million pounds or so needed for updating the mainframe,

which was always nodded through'. A more robust, a more pluralist, system of democratic debate and scrutiny would surely have produced a challenge to this state of affairs.

The impact of the city-wide political and trade union campaign to keep council services in council hands revived political pluralism, mainly as a result of dissenting voices in the Labour Group having the courage and determination to speak out. A proportional electoral system would help to build this pluralism and debate into local government. Certainly, it is a question that needs to be discussed as part of developing effective strategies for publicly led public service change.

Whether or not electoral reform is introduced, scrutiny of local government needs to be strengthened. But the present mechanisms of scrutiny are too weak, under-resourced and removed from the wider public to be an adequate check on local decision-making. Much more needs to be done to make local accountability a reality, any scrutiny and participation mechanisms should be used to bring to bear the pressure of local politicians - along with user and community groups, trade unions, and engaged citizens - on developing local services in a positive and progressive way.

## The importance of public services in securing the future

Writing up this story of efficiency in the public sector at a time when the financial edifices created by neo-liberal economics, are collapsing all about us, brings home the true importance of the welfare state and the urgency of its renewal and reconstruction.

The reform of Newcastle council's ICT services shows in a very practical way how the public sector can have its own criteria of efficiency, distinct from goals of profit. The livelihoods and communities of millions of people stand in need of protection from the misjudgements of those with both political and economic power. This story adds to an already considerable body of evidence that local government has the capacity to make itself an effective steward of public money.[16]

At present the government's approach to public spending is defensive. There is an inbuilt bias towards outsourcing, even though this means that a percentage of savings is taken away as profit, and there is no recognition of the possibility for councils to expand services and create new jobs once efficiencies have been achieved. Yet surely new jobs could usefully be created by the public sector throughout the UK - in caring services, youth services, environmental services, ICT, strengthening the social economy … it is not as though there is a lack of things that need doing!

Recessions are accompanied by social devastation. One foundation stone of a new more humane political economy should be the expansion of a democratically reformed public sector.

I rest my case!

# Public service reform . . . but not as we know it!

1. Newcastle council scored highest in 2007/8 amongst cities such as Manchester, Leeds, Birmingham, Liverpool, Bristol etc. for time taken to process claims, on CIPFA measures. The average time take to process a claim fell from 40 to less than 20 days in 2003.

2. Satisfaction with the cashiers' services (the ways in which people pay council tax and rent) have gone up to 98% from 78% in 2006. 90% of users had their queries solved at the first point of contact - the target was 80%. A weekly average of 7,650 people use the Customer Service Centres – the third highest in the benchmarking group.

3. Newcastle have moved from being at the lower end of the league of major cities on collection of council tax to the upper, collecting over 2 % more in 2007/8 than in 2005/6.

4. Net of investment, for example on new IT hardware and voluntary redundancy payments.

5. Department of Communities and Local Government and Local Government Association. Several parts of the council aim to support ' community empowerment' but the Contact Centre and the Customer Service Centres contribute indirectly to strengthening citizens' control over council policy and resources by improving their day to day access to council staff and services and by involving community organisations in determining strategy.

6. We saw in Chapter 8 how City Service ICT service for schools, after originally being barred from bidding under the government's Building Schools for the Future for the contract for Newcastle's schools (because it was public sector), went on get the second highest score in the Audit commission's annual survey of schools. It was the major source of an expansion of City Service to 653 staff. Thus although the transformation programme involved a reduction of 153 of the original posts, it also led to new posts working for an improved service carrying out new functions improving the quality of education.

7. Council staff and community organiser both say that there is more to be done to strengthen citizens participation in many aspects of council decision-making.

8. City Service's wide range of methods for paying council tax or rent (online, by telephone, in person, by cheque, by card) and places for paying (Customer Service Centres, newsagents, grocers, post offices) show that a highly personalised service can be provided by a public authority, once it has been reorganised to make identifying and meeting the needs and desires of its users its first priority. Choice may not always be the key issue providing good public service, however, but rather the ability to meet the individual, personal needs of those who use it - see Adam Lent and Natalie Arend, *Making Choices: How can choice improve local public services?* New Local Government Network, 2004. http://www.nlgn.org.uk/pdfs/upload/Making%20Choices%20summary.pdf

9. Through participatory budgeting, popular involvement in planning decisions and in policies for regeneration.

10. A report by the Prime Minister's Strategy Unit admits the possibility that two factors now generally seen as important for efficiency - collaborative practices and public service ethics - might be weakened by outsourcing. It dismisses this by asserting without empirical evidence that 'the risks to collaboration posed by competition need to be weighed against the benefits of competition in terms of stimulating innovation and the diffusion of best practice'. The report does not consider the possibility of other stimuli to innovation or other means of diffusing good practice more appropriate to the public sector – such as democratic pressure from citizens' participation, more plural forms of electoral politics, more open creative styles of management and more engagement of the workforce. It draws on *Motivation, Agency and Public Policy*, 2003, the work of one of the main proponents of 'competition and contestability' Julian le Grand who takes the pubic service ethos as a static given and does not consider conditions that might enliven it or make it more effective.

11. An interesting study by Professor Peter deSouza ( www.idea.int/sod) uses the economic term 'transaction costs' to suggest that studies of democracy should seek to measure the transaction costs of claiming entitlements, benefits or services from the state to assess how far public institutions provide an everyday experience of democracy. Quoted in an unpublished paper by Stuart Weir, Director of Democratic Audit, 'Engaging *with* the Public: people's everyday experience of democracy' .stuart.weir2@ntlworld.com

12. Of course public services are not the same as the subject matter of physics! It is an understanding of key relationships, mechanisms, principles and values that we can draw from the City Service story, not universal laws. Indeed one of the lessons of the story is how attentive reform strategies must be to the specifics of the service, the institutions and their histories to be effective.

13. For a useful discussion of ways of leading change unbureacratically see 'Leading Change' A forthcoming paper by Su Maddock from the Whitehall Innovation Hub.

14. This point is reinforced by a very interesting paper on what public service reform can learn from social movements, Paul Bate, Helen Bevan and Glenn Robert, *Towards a Million Change Agents*, NHS Modernisation Agency, 2004. http://eprints.ucl.ac.uk/1133/1/million.pdf. This paper puts emphasis on the importance of an 'animating vision' that can motivate people and bind them together so that they can act in a coordinated but innovative (non procedure-bound) way.

15. See 'Partnership and Productivity in the Public Sector: A Review of the Literature' report by Brendan Martin of The Partnership Resource Centre.

16. See Davy Jones ' Looking Back, Going Forward' IDeA/LGA Febuary 2009; Dave Prentis, 'Look Before You Leap', *Public Finance*, 9 January 2009.

# Chronology

| | |
|---|---|
| 1999 | A joint venture with the private sector is proposed for the IT and Related Services (ITRS) of Newcastle City Council |
| July 2000 | UNISON branch 'awayday' to discuss the increasing pressure to privatise and work out strategy for defending public services and campaigning for 'in-house' alternatives to outsourcing. |
| August 2000 | UNISON branch writes to Newcastle City Council chief executive declaring its opposition to outsourcing the work of ITRS to private firms |
| December 2000 | UNISON branch publishes Outsourcing the Future: a Social and Economic Audit of Outsourcing Proposals in Newcastle with the Centre for Public Services.(CPS) |
| 2001 | Regular mass meetings of ITRS staff |
| 2001 | Ballot of ITRS staff which shows overwhelming support for industrial action against outsourcing |
| September 2001 | Industrial action by ITRS staff called off at last minute after City Council obtains injunction but rally went ahead as planned. |
| October 2001 | Labour Group meets and agrees resolution supporting in-house services and rejecting privatisation unless all in-house alternatives explored. |
| May 002 | Joint union/management workshop in support of in-house bid |
| September 2002 | The council accepts the in-house option |
| October 2002 | The council agrees to the creation of City Service to take over and transform the ITRS division |
| November 2002 | The Customer Relationship Management IT system is introduced |
| April 2003 | The new City Service management team begins work |

| | |
|---|---|
| Early 2003 | PA consulting working with City Service on Programme Management Plan. |
| June 2003 | First meeting of City Service Transformation Board |
| August 2003 | The first customer service centre (CSC) outside the civic centre opens – this and all subsequent CSCs awarded Charter Mark for service. |
| December 2003 | Guaranteed Maximum Price contract signed between Newcastle Council and Fujitsu |
| March 2004 | Exchequer billing and invoicing systems rationalised |
| May 2004 | The Liberal Democrats win control of Newcastle City Council from Labour |
| October 2004 | The council's customer service strategy is revised and expanded |
| October 2004 | Awarded the Achievement Award from the British Computer Society for the implementation of CRM |
| October 2004 | Win the Association of Public Sector Employees award for innovation and IT in Service Delivery |
| November 2004 | Win the Northern Region Business Achievement award for CRM |
| November 2004 | SAP (the new payroll system) goes live with redesigned jobs and structure |
| November 2004 | The council's benefits staff are moved from 21 neighbourhood offices to a new, central office near to the civic centre |
| December 2004 | New system (SX3) for national non-domestic rates went live |
| April – May 2005 | Physical to electronic scanning of documents went live in benefits and revenues |
| June – August 2005 | Other key systems went live concerned with housing and also with integrating the Customer Relationship Management (CRM) system with new council tax system |

## Public service reform . . . but not as we know it!

| | |
|---|---|
| September 2005 | Regional Winners of National Business Award - business improvement through people |
| February 2006 | A new 'payment engine' is introduced providing a single view of all financial transactions, new cashiering system and allowing customers to make payments for council tax and other council services on line and through self service telephony. |
| February 2006 | New system for council tax and benefits (SX3 ) went live |
| March 2006 | The new  contact centre opens at the civic centre |
| April/May 2006 | Decision to replace Document Management System |
| December 2006 | The old mainframe computer that hosted all of the Councils business applications is decommissioned |
| January 2007 | Replacement Document Management System live in revenues and benefits |
| July 2007 | City Service wins contract for ICT services for Newcastle's schools, leading to an expansion City Service activity and employment. It is the first public sector bid allowed under Schools for the Future, after being initially refused, |
| Nov 2007 | City Service awarded Investor In People status |
| 2008 | Successful completion of  improvement and savings goals set out in the in-house bid |
| November 2008 | Last of six customer service centres opens in Benwell, west end of the city. |
| 2008 - | Ray Ward, Kath Moore and most of the  City Service Development and Transformation team take on  the wider challenge of transforming the council as a whole. |
| 2008 – 2009 | UNISON Newcastle branch and Newcastle Council agree an approach to service reform based on in-house improvement plans and where an alternative provider is being considered, the development of in-house bids and a key role for the trade unions in the procurement and commissioning process. |

UNISON Northern Region adopts a strategy for all public services based on the Newcastle experience, combining campaigning against outsourcing with in-house improvement plans and where necessary, in-house bids. See www.unison.org.uk/northern

UNISON nationally produces guidance on campaigns and negotiations over procurement and commissioning drawing on the Newcastle experience.

# About the authors

**Hilary Wainwright** is a Fellow of the Transnational Institute in Amsterdam, Senior Research Associate of the International Centre for Participation Studies, Bradford University and Co-editor of *Red Pepper*. Her other books include *A Workers Report on Vickers* with Huw Beynon (1979) *Beyond the Fragments, Feminism and the Making of Socialism* with Sheila Rowbotham and Lynne Segal (1981) *The Lucas Story, A New Trade Unionism in the Making?* with Dave Elliott (1982), *Labour, A Tale of Two Parties* (1988) *Arguments for a New Left, Answering the Free Market Right* (1994) *Reclaim the State, Experiments in Popular Democracy* (2003 and update 2009)

**Mat Little** is a writer and freelance journalist who write a weekly column in Third Sector and contributes to the Guardian on public and third sector issues.

# Methodology and acknowledgements

This is an inside story written on the basis of intensive interviews with people involved in every aspect and level of the process of change. Also we had discussions with groups of ten or so staff in every section of City Service, who volunteered for the purpose.

The management of City Service, the political leadership and managers of the council, the city council branch of UNISON all gave us their full co-operation. Most of the research was done during March, April and May 2008. I spent these months based in the Civic Centre. (I was given a vast empty room to squat in as the room awaited its official occupants.) Mat Little spent a month in Newcastle, in the Civic, and talking to community organisations in the city.

Over the summer 2008 we wrote a first draft. Mat wrote the sections on the public's experiences of City Service before and after the transformation. These are in chapter 1 and chapter 8. He wrote about the creation and workings of the Customer Service Centres in chapter 8 and about the redeployment and retraining programme in chapter 9. I wrote the rest, with much useful feedback from Mat.

The draft was then sent to everyone interviewed, and to others with expertise on public service improvement. There was a three month period of feedback and discussion from the middle of September until mid December 2008. During this time I returned to Newcastle on several occasions to discuss the draft with City Service and with UNISON, and to conduct further interviews. A day long seminar was held to discuss the draft and contribute to the conclusions. At this seminar were; Kenny Bell, Josie Bird and Lisa Marshall from UNISON's city council branch; Ray Ward and Julia Woollard from City Service; Su Maddock from the Whitehall Innovation Hub, Dexter Whitfield from European Services Strategy Unit, Martin Mcivor a national UNISON policy officer, Malcolm Wing and Mark Bramagh from APSE and Daniel Chavez from the Transnational Institute. It was facilitated by Keith Hodgson the education officer of the Northern Region of UNISON who also gave me an interview on the union's intensive work on shop steward training and his impressions of the city council branch.

All the participants individually have given me very useful comments, suggestions and references. Here I want especially to thank Martin McIvor, Dexter Whitfield and Malcolm Wing for their sustained support and regular suggestions. (I'm sorry they won't see everything they suggested as it would have doubled the size of the book!)

I also received very helpful comments from Heather Wakefield head of UNISON's Local Government section, Margie Jaffe, Head of UNISON's Positively Public Campaign and Simon Watson, National Officer for the UNISON Local Government Service Group.

The more we investigated, the more we realised how exemplary, in its difficulties as well as its successes, is the Newcastle story and how full of insights for others working to improve public services. We decided in consultation with UNISON and City Service management that it was important to explain the detail. Because Newcastle council management and union give first priority to supporting the people who work for City Service and to meeting the needs of those it is intended to serve, we have tried to do likewise. The detail of the story has involved highlighting the views and experiences of the people who worked together to make it a success, as well as those who use Newcastle's services, and as a result the book is longer than we originally anticipated. We hope that nevertheless, you find it readable and enjoyable,

# Public service reform . . . but not as we know it!

as well as a useful source of knowledge. The final draft has been expertly edited by Steve Platt who is undoubtedly one of the best editors around. As the project expanded in words and time, Steve was ably abetted by Hilary Bichovsky who has a special touch. I want to thank them both for their patience and their skill.

On a personal note, I'm grateful to my mother, Joyce Wainwright, for amongst other things, providing a welcoming stop-over in Leeds on the regular return journeys from Newcastle to Manchester; and to Roy Bhaskar for providing a sounding board on philosophical matters.

I also want to thank Jen Nelson, Phil Dennison, Lorna Tittle and Andrea D' Cruz for painstakingly transcribing pages of in depth interviews. And Jane Foot and Judith Green for reading an earlier draft and giving me useful comments. I want to give a special thanks to Julia Woollard, who was the programme manager for the City Service transformation and who almost acted as a programme manager for the book, reading every draft, making corrections and many wise comments with immense good will and cheerful encouragement. The book also owes a huge amount to the commitment and sparky intelligence of Josie Bird, chair of the UNISON city branch who organised the discussion groups, read the manuscript in full, giving me useful comments and criticisms that deepened my analysis of the role of the union. I also want to thank Sue Praszczalek and everyone in the Newcastle Branch office for giving us their support. In the final production of the book,I owe much to the designer , John Schwartz for his skill and his calm. I want to pay a special tribute to Kenny Bell for understanding the wider importance of what his trade union branch, the staff and management of City Service had done, and obtaining the resources for the story to be told and the wider lessons highlighted and publicised.

I want to thank Ray Ward and City Service staff and ex-staff most notably Fred Stephen and Jeff Pasternack for their patience as we pestered them with our questions; Barry Rowland, now the council's acting chief executive and John Shipley, leader of the council, for their wholehearted and unconditional support for the study .

I must take responsibility for all mistakes or controversial judgements. My main aim has been to show that democratically driven public service change is an effective, proven alternative to outsourcing and privatisation; and to do all I could to push it into the centre of public policy and trade union strategy.

I feel in some respects the story deserves to be studied at greater depth! But there is an urgency in getting it out, discussed and learnt from. Hopefully it will encourage others to share their experiences so that public democratic drivers of change become in practice the common sense of public service improvement.

Please give us your feedback, your questions, doubts, criticism and your own experiences. Write to Kenny Bell or me at unison.newcastle@newcastle.gov.uk. We hope to set up an online forum on the issues raised by the book to take forward strategies for public, democratic public service reform.

**Hilary Wainwright**, Manchester. February 2009.

# Compass

Compass is the democratic left pressure group whose goal is both to debate and develop the ideas for a more equal and democratic society, then campaign and organise to help ensure they become reality. We organise regular events and conferences that provide real space to discuss policy, we produce thought provoking pamphlets, and we encourage debate through online discussions on our website. We campaign, take positions and lead the debate on key issues facing the democratic left. We're developing a coherent and strong voice for those that believe in greater equality and democracy as the means to achieve radical social change.

We are:

- An umbrella grouping of the progressive left whose sum is greater than its parts.
- A strategic political voice - unlike thinktanks and single-issue pressure groups Compass can develop a politically coherent position based on the values of equality and democracy.
- An organising force - Compass recognises that ideas need to be organised for, and will seek to recruit, mobilise and encourage to be active a membership across the UK to work in pursuit of greater equality and democracy.
- A pressure group focused on changing Labour - but Compass recognises that energy and ideas can come from outside the party, not least from the 200,000 who have left since 1997.
- The central belief of Compass is that things will only change when people believe they can and must make a difference themselves. In the words of Gandhi: 'Be the change you wish to see in the world'.

## compass

# Positively Public

Positively Public is UNISON's campaign for quality in our public services, and for recognition of the essential role of public service workers in achieving this. Positively Public has campaigned on a range of public service issues, from the quality of school meals and hospital cleaning to the promotion of best practice. UNISON has pursued a twin track approach to public service campaigning that opposes the privatisation and marketisation of public services in principle but also recognises that where reforms are going ahead, UNISON must get the best protections for its members.

UNISON's Positively Public campaign has won widespread recognition and support for our evidence-based critiques of policies such as the Private Finance Initiative and have been successful in securing a number of important policy changes.

For more information and to access briefings and research reports, visit **www.unison.org.uk/positivelypublic**

To get in touch or sign up for regular briefings and alerts email positivelypublic@unison.co.uk

# The Transnational Institute

Founded in 1974, the Transnational Institute (TNI) is an international network of activist-scholars committed to critical analyses of the global problems of today and tomorrow, with a view to providing intellectual support to those movements concerned to steer the world in a democratic, equitable and environmentally sustainable direction.

In the spirit of public scholarship, and aligned to no political party, TNI seeks to create and promote international co-operation in analysing and finding possible solutions to such global problems as militarism and conflict, poverty and marginalisation, social injustice and environmental degradation.

email: tni@tni.org
website: www.tni.org

T
N
I

# International Centre for Participation Studies

The International Centre for Participation Studies was created in 2003 to provide a focus for research and teaching on the relationship between political participation and peace. ICPS is based in the Department of Peace Studies at the University of Bradford, the largest academic centre for the study of peace and conflict in the world. ICPS provides a space for critical reflection, education and research on all aspects of participatory theory and practice, informed by a commitment to collective action for peace. Our research links theory and practice to explore how participation is thought about and utilised and our work involves practitioners in the co-production of this knowledge. We work at the local, regional and global levels and have extensive links to partner organisations including other academic institutions, local and regional government, NGOs, community organisations and social movements. We have extensive research interests in the North of England and Latin America and an established research profile in East Africa.

website: www.brad.ac.uk/acad/icps